Four Cultures of Education
Engineer – Expert – Communicator – Prophet

STUDIES IN PEDAGOGY, ANDRAGOGY AND GERONTOLOGY

edited by Franz Pöggeler

Vol. 18

PETER LANG

Frankfurt am Main · Berlin · Bern · New York · Paris · Wien

Walter Leirman

Four Cultures of Education

Expert, Engineer, Prophet, Communicator

PETER LANG

Europäischer Verlag der Wissenschaften

Die Deutsche Bibliothek - CIP-Einheitsaufnahme

Leirman, Walter:

Four cultures of education : engineer, expert, communicator,
prophet / Walter Leirman. - Frankfurt am Main ; Berlin ; Bern ;
New York ; Paris ; Wien : Lang, 1994
    (Studien zur Pädagogik, Andragogik und Gerontagogik ;
    Bd. 18)
    Einheitssacht.: Vier culturen van educatie <engl.>
    ISBN 3-631-47097-5

Title of original edition: Vier culturen van educatie,
Leuven-Apeldoorn, Garant, 1993

CL   370
  cl   c.1

ISSN 0934-3695
ISBN 3-631-47097-5

© Peter Lang GmbH
Europäischer Verlag der Wissenschaften
Frankfurt am Main 1994
All rights reserved.

Printed in Germany 1 2 3   5 6 7

CONTENT

PREFACE

A book is not a fruit-of-one-season. The first thoughts for the present book emerged four years ago, during a discussion with colleagues at an international conference on "education and the state" in Germany. We were discussing several concepts and existing systems of education in different countries. What struck me was not only the diversity of positions and opinions in the group, but even more the fairly stereotypical way in which participants talked about other countries and other systems of thought. Thus, the labels "modern", "outdated" and "post-modern" were used lavishly. I then decided to look deeper into the matter of different approaches to and different practices of education.

A book is (mostly) not a single person's product either. Having set up a general synopsis for the present book, I presented it at a conference celebrating prof. J. Knoll's 60th birthday in Germany, and then sent a copy to several colleagues, with a request for further suggestions. I received useful materials from L. Vandemeule-broecke, D. Wildemeersch and H. Baert at my own department, and from colleagues from other departments of Education and Psychology at the K.U. Leuven, namely R. Bouwen, M. Depaepe, K. De Witte, P. Smeyers, R. Vandenberghe, L. Verschaffel and W. Wielemans. They all belong to my "flemish professional circle", and I thank them for their contribution. But this book would not have come about if I had not been able to draw upon the expertise and experience of foreign colleagues and groups as well. I want to mention, in the first place, our *Erasmus-group* with F. Pöggeler (Aachen), P. Jarvis (Surrey), T. Jansen (Nijmegen), R. Flecha (Barcelona) and P. Hébrard (Montpellier). Secondly, there is the core group of our *International Institute for Policy, Practice and Research in the education of adults*, with O. Feinstein (Wayne state), E. Bockstael (Louvain-la-neuve-), K. Forrester (Leeds), B. Cave (Univ. of Michigan) and W. Uegama (British Columbia).

Two further circumstances have been crucial in the writing process: the fact that the academic authorities of the K.U. Leuven gave me a sabbatical leave - partly based on the plan signalled above -, and the fact that I found a haven of silence and good care in the monastery of the Franciscan Friar Minors in Vaalbeek (Belgium). I thank both instances for their facilitating efforts. At the same time, I thank my secretary Marc Vlecken for his invaluable logistic support.

Finally, I wish to thank my wife Angela, my closest ally and attentive critical reader. This book is about four cultures. She is the basis of my fifth culture!

Walter Leirman
September 1993

INTRODUCTION: THE PARADOXES OF EDUCATION

One of the well-known jokes in circles of adult education tells the following story: a middle-aged man came to tell the director of an educational centre "Sir, I'm so confused these days, I don't know what to think. Could you please help me?" The director looked at his programme brochure and advised him to take a course on "Modern thinkers about modern man". After the course, the man came to see the director again. "Well, are you still confused?" The adult student answered: "Yes, sir, I am still confused, but at a higher level"... In post-modern times, the joke might well end differently: "Yes, sir, but I am now confused at a deeper level: I have found out that confusion is the basic mode of existence".

At the end of the twentieth century, people working in or concerned with all forms of education are confronted with profound uncertainties. In an era which is being called "post-modern" or "late modern", we seem to have lost any sense of direction. Goals, contents, methods, outcomes are becoming increasingly unclear, or, at least, extremely diverse. The French author Lyotard stated recently that "the time of the Great Discourses and ideologies is over", and that statement has found many echoes. Professionals of education - educators as well as policy makers and scientists - are being told to give up their dreams and frameworks, and to go and listen carefully to what "the common people" have to say.

In democracy, wisdom, they say, lies with the people. Let us, therefore listen to them. Careful listening has brought colleagues and myself to the finding that people have very diverse opinions about education of man and woman in today's world indeed: some refer to education as a means to instill values and beliefs, some others see it as the developer of rational thinking and solid knowledge, whereas some others talk about education as the provider of professional skills, or, on the contrary, as the excavator of slumbering potentialities.

The most common denominator in people's thinking about education is, however, that education means *production of different cultural goods*, which one acquires at home and especially at school, and which allow the "educated" to cope with their personal and social problems. "Get yourself a good education" is a standard message to young and old in many places in the world.

I would like to make a first comment on this standard belief in education by means of an analogy. It is taken from the world of wine and wine-making. Wine too is seen as an end-product, "made" at a chateau, a bodega or a winery, and owing its quality above all to the technical interventions of its maker. After eight thousand years of practice, we even have a science of wine-making, called "oenology" (from greek "oinos = wine" and "logos = knowledge"). The media, especially wine magazines, are spreading the message that "good wine is the product of a good wine-maker, using modern techniques".

This message contains little truth, because it tells only the last part of a long story. Good wine is only made from good grapes. Grapes grow on vines planted in a vineyard, during a season, which starts with the burgeoning of fresh leaves in early spring, and ends with the ripening of the bunches in early autumn. That process is highly dependent upon sun and soil on the one hand, and on the continuous care of the "viticulteur" on the other hand. One can only say that "cultivating grapes" is a process of complex interaction between nature and man. To see man as "wine-maker" is, in fact, an overstatement. A well-known oenologist from Bordeaux once told me: 'it is undeniable that modern technology plays an increasingly important role in the process of wine-making, yet there is a definite limit to technical intervention. We are in fact operating within a triangle: nature, technique and care. Only the combination of these three can explain why each year, each winery, and even sometimes each bottle brings a different wine".

Educa-tor rimes with *viticul-tor*: makability has long been at the core of concepts and practices of education. And the most simple reason for that is that man and society itself was seen as "makable".

Where did humanity get this "constructivist" belief? Some historians of education point to the 17th and 18th centuries, the times of Enlightenment, Aufklärung and "L'âge de la Raison". Did not Michel de Montaigne, in his essay 'De l'institution des enfants' (1572) state that people had to learn to think rationally and independently, and that the actual practices of education were too much like "the filling of brains" or "pouring contents down a funnel" ? And what did Kant state in his famous essay on the nature of Enlightenment ('was ist aufklärung', 1783): "Aufklärung is the process by means of which man steps out of his self-induced lack of emancipation ('unmündigkeit')... meaning the impotence to use one's own brains without the help of others... Take courage and use your brains!".

The practices criticized by these authors are intriguingly depicted by our Renaissance painter Pieter Breugel, in a scene from his series on popular sayings, drawn in 1557. The saying illustrated here is the following (transl.): "even if a donkey travels to school to learn, being a donkey, he will not return as a learned horse". That donkey appears in the upper left corner, staring in bewilderment at a music score. The candle and the pair of glasses painted to the left and the right refer to yet another well-known proverb (transl.): "of what avail are glasses and candle, if the owl does not want to handle ?"

The question is, however, whether the ironic Breugel wanted only to illustrate the popular saying. The central figure in the picture is the school teacher, who is castigating one of the children, perhaps because it did not do its best, or was simply too dumb. Within this framework, education is seen indeed as en-light-enment, the light coming from books and tables, to which pupils are "uplifted" by the central figure of the schoolmaster. And if pupils are unwilling to listen to his instructions, they are "taught by the hard hand".

PARISIOS STOLIDVM SI QVIS TRANSMITTAT ASELLVM · SI HIC EST ASINVS NON ERIT ILLIC EQVVS ·
Al reyst den cfele ter sisolen om leeren ist eenen esele hij eg sal gheen peert weder keeren

Figure 1: Pieter Breugel the Elder (1557) "If a donkey goes to school.."

Statements like those made by de Montaigne and Kant are in fact imbedded in a broad cultural, social and political climate, which is literally symbolized by Columbus' discovery of "the New World". 'Our time has written more history in one hundred years, than the whole world in four thousand years before.' These are not the words of the Nobel prize committee, but of Tommaso Campanella, writing in the year 1623.[1] His conviction was shared by many other authors, the most influential of whom may well have been Francis Bacon. His utopian story of *New Atlantis* (1627) reveals the promised land of the human *ratio*, organiser of systematic experiments, leading to 'the effecting of all things possible'. On the cover of another book, *Instauratio magna* (1620), he let an artist depict the dynamics of the "pertransitio" of science:

---

[1] We are making use here of the introduction to the publication <u>Wetenschap Nu en Morgen</u> (Science, today and tomorrow) published in 1989 under the editorship of Paul De Meester, Roger Dillemans e.a. by Leuven University Press. This book contains a "status questionis" of the different scientific disciplines. We ourselves contributed to the chapter on educational sciences.

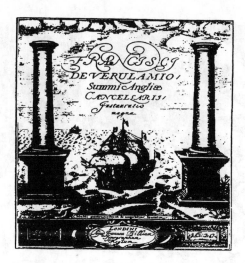

Figure 2:
Cover page of F.
Bacon's   Instau-
ratio magna

The outer framework of the picture consists of two columns of Hercules or Heracle, which, from ancient Greece through the Middle Ages, symbolised the limits of the world. But these columns now become the gates of a seaport, where huge ships come and go. The statement written under the incoming ship translates it clearly: "many will make the passage, and science will flourish" .

However, the picture of solid land and moving sea has another symbolic meaning: the times of Bacon are the times of a radical confrontation between the classical, especially Greek tradition and the new, "enlightened" ways of Renaissance. The Greek "natural" philosophers were the first in trying to develop a systematical and rational explanation of natural phenomena, declaring, e.g. that the pushing power of trade winds caused the yearly flooding of the Nile. The "theatre of the Gods" thus became a "theatre of human rationality". That tradition culminated in the works of Plato and Aristotle.

For those of us who are troubled by the present-day debate between "modernists" and "post-modernists", it is illuminating to look back at the debates which were carried on in ancient Greece. For the development of "modern" science in general, and of the science of education in particular, it is of great importance to look into the distinction made between (aristotelian) physics and mechanics. At that time, physics was a philosophical study of the fundaments of the "natural order": the characteristics of natural phenomena, their operations and changes and the relationship between the outer form and the inner essence. Physics in ancient Greece were non-experimental and non-mathematical. Mechanics, on the other hand, were (and are) empirically and practically oriented. Thus, Archimedes observed the working of levers, and formulated the principles behind it, so that they could be applied in many areas. Mechanics were a practical, or in modern parlance, an applied science. There is a German/Dutch duet of verbs that helps to explain this difference: *BE-greifen/BE-grijpen* versus *EIN-greifen/IN-grijpen*. Greek physics wanted to UNDER-stand, Greek mechanics wanted to INTER-vene. Physics focused on defining the LOGOS, i.e. the immanent reason governing nature, whereas mechanics were focusing on TECHNE, i.e. the art of using and manipulating natural objects.

In the eyes of the Greek, there were, however, clear limits to the power of technique: TECHNE could only *imitate* nature, but never equal, let alone *change* it or *create* new realities.

The Greek were not only the founders of rational science, but also the creators of the POLIS, the city-state, for which Athens served as a prototype. For the government of the city (Poli-tics), i.e. for the exertion of power, public debate played a central role. To debate was not to exchange ritual phrases or coined expressions, but to discuss before an audience, which gathered in the public space or agora, and served as a referee. Some even state that human rationality came to the forefront, not through the work of philosophers and scientists, but through the practice of argumentative debating in the Greek polis. The rules of the debate became, later on, the rules of the scientific game.

It should not take wonder, therefore, that education in ancient Greece was conceived of as "the preparation and training of good citizens". However, in speaking of the Greek tradition, we should neither idealise nor oversimplify things. One city-state was not like another: in Sparta, the focus was on physical training, handicrafts and military discipline, and government was strongly centralised, whereas in Athens, the accent was put on rearing well-balanced personalities, both in the intellectual, the moral and the physical sense of the word, and with far less state interference. The arts played barely any role in Sparta - with the exception of Homer's war poetry - whereas Athens payed great attention to music and drama. On the other hand, Spartans offered educational opportunities to their girls and women, whereas Athens restricted women's education to a training in housekeeping in the family home. In both cities, education was not restricted to youth, but adults received further education. Contrary to the "modern" belief that adult education started around the First Industrial Revolution, ancient Greece developed its own system of adult education. (Grattan, 1955)

The great philosophers all payed strong attention to education. Thus, Plato's *Republic*, often held to be a political treatise, is in the first place a profound essay on education. And his pupil Aristotle opened the last chapter of his *Politics* as follows: 'No one will doubt that the legislator should direct his attention above all to the education of youth...The citizen should be moulded to suit the form of government under which he lives'. Yet again, both authors differed in their opinion about the relationship between the individual, the family and the city-state: Plato, having witnessed the tragic trial and death of his master Socrates, favoured a communal system of education, with elimination of the family and parental control, whereas Aristotle was sceptical of this kind of commonwealth and saw the family as the nucleus of personal development and well-being. He pleaded for an education towards "social individuality".

Yet, both authors strongly agreed about the *ethical basis* of education. In his treatise on Laws, Plato gives a straightforward answer to the question of the real meaning of education: "If you ask what is generally good in education, the answer is easy: education produces good men, and good men act nobly". Such statements again found a convincing experiential basis in the life and the teachings of Socrates. Socrates, who saw the endless ramifications of so-called logical thinkers - the mongers of sophistry -, put a very strong accent on ethics and "knowledge of the good soul", which should beware of wealth, power and distraction. Furthermore, Socrates did not believe so much in the necessity to "mould" individuals, but far more in the unfolding of innate capacities and wisdom. He used the "profession" of his mother, who acted as a "midwife", as a metaphor for the role of the educator: he ought to act as a "maieutic" who sets free a person's inborn qualities and helps to shape them.

*   *   *

Our starting point - the confusion about (adult) education in the so-called post-modern era - seems to find its mirror in the practices of and the reflections on education in ancient Greece: we find "instrumental" concepts next to "dialogical" concepts, a stress on "truth" as the main goal direction versus an accent on "goodness" or the combination of both, a preference for "individualism" versus a focus on "communalism", social selectivity in favour of an "academically trained elite" in Athens versus "education for all" in Sparta, a centralist policy in more "military regimes" versus a decentralised policy in a more "democratic" regime.

Our common image of the cultural and educational system in ancient Greece is, however, far less diversified. To many of us, ancient Greece stands for rationalism and individualism on the one hand, and immersion in mythology on the other.

The reason for this narrowed view may very well be found in our "modern" tradition: we are the children of the 17th and 18th centuries, of the rationalism of Descartes, the atomism of Newton, the autonomism of Kant. At the same time, that "modern" tradition, and its products - a welfare state, a competitive free market, a fragmented world of science, a Declaration of (personal) Human Rights, an individual-oriented system of education - are under heavy criticism and/or under revision.

Among the many signals of this "post-modern" debate, I would like to point to a very public one, at least within one country and via one medium. I am referring to a series of TV-programmes broadcast in English by the VPRO-television in the Netherlands in the autumn and the winter of 1992-93, under the title "A Glorious Accident". The leader of this series, Wim Kayzer, invited six scientists with a world reputation in their respective fields, first to individual interviews, and finally, to a concluding one-day "round table" discussion about some of the major issues raised during the previous interviews. The interview partners were: Oliver Sacks, neurologist; Rupert Sheldrake, biochemist; Daniel G. Dennett, philosopher; Stephen Toulmin, philosopher of science; Freeman Dyson, physicist; Stephen Jay Gould, paleontologist.

The title for the series referred to a quotation from Gould's book on evolution: 'That we, through no fault of our own, and by dent of no cosmic plan or conscious purpose, have become, by the power of a Glorious evolutionary Accident called Intelligence, the stewards of life on earth'.

In the conversation, as it was synthesised in a 4 hour-long programme (!), all partners, with the exception of R. Sheldrake, agreed with this view on radical contingency or arbitrariness of evolution of the planet. They still agreed when confronted with the following synthesis of Charles Darwin's theory of evolution:

(1) evolution has no purpose
(2) matter is the ground of all existence
(3) evolution is not a gradual process
(4) evolution has no direction.

However, D. Dennett made a very important correction: evolution is not simply what goes on in the cosmos, but it is inextricably linked to the transmission of human culture: "culture introduced self-determination in the biological process" (Kayzer, 1993)

For our purposes, the interview with Steven Toulmin, physicist and philosopher, was very illuminating. In his most recent work, Cosmopolis, he states that the adventure of modernity is stranded: 'with eyes lowered, we are backing into a new millennium'. The project of modernity was basically initiated by Descartes and Newton. Descartes equated consciousness with the human brain, and developed the art of being rational by universal application of the so-called scientific method. He was the father of mathematical physics - a very positive contribution - but also of the "cartesian theatre of rational man" - a deplorable mistake. The transition of the world of, say, Thomas Aquinas and that of Descartes became literally visible in what happened in the world of the theatre between 1600 and 1640. William Shakespeare still operated in the *apron stage* of the theatre, showing "slices of real life", allowing the audience to really "recognise part of themselves". Around 1640, "modern" theatre made its appearance in the form of the *proscenium*. Here, a curtain was set up between the players and the audience, and theatre was about a "mysterious, hidden world", which the author would unfold to the public...

The cartesian trap was the idea that "the world begins in the mind of Descartes". Newton further developed this line of thought, with his project of explaining all reality by way of a set of equations and "eternal" laws. In philosophy, said Toulmin, we had to wait for somebody like Ludwig Wittgenstein, to take us away from the illusion that we can explain everything, that everything is predictable and reality is "well-ordered". He also pointed out that both Descartes and Newton had an unhappy childhood, being deprived very early in their lives, of parental care.

Asked about his major worry, S. Toulmin stated that he was baffled by the tendency of humans to violence and destruction - and he referred thereby to the many wars that are being fought today, especially the one in former Yugoslavia. He added that the statement that "nothing can ever surpass the annihilation of 6 million Jews in World War II" is simply a myth, and that 45 years of efforts at peacemaking via politics, the media or education had not been of much avail.

That statement was presented to the other colleagues in the round table discussion, and there the answer was less pessimistic: S. Young said that, in comparison to the animal world, the world of humans is far less destructive and, on the whole, very peaceful. One of the problems, he said, is our concept of news as purveyed by the media. One of the factors behind the "peacefulness" of humans seemed to be the transmission of moral standards via the family and the school. But that statement was contradicted by several partners, who stated that present-day education was far too a-moral, teaching children that "the other is your competitor".

In this TV-series, the science of education (pedagogy/andragogy) was not repre-sented, and references to education were scarce. This fact can be interpreted in several ways:
a) pedagogy/andragogy is not considered to be a "full-fledged" science but rather a field of practice ;
b) the present-day scientific agenda does not list educational questions as important;
c) pedagogy/andragogy is too young as a discipline and has to grow and develop ;
d) pedagogy/andragogy is in itself too isolated and also too divided over its different currents and action fields to become a partner in a broad multi-disciplinary debate.

We ourselves think that all four explanations are partially valid, including the latter one. It maybe consoling to note that several representatives of other disciplines in the discussion, especially philosophy, applied some of these judgments to their own field. And the youngest of them all, a physicist, stated that "today's science is unpopular, because it is seen as one of the major contributors to our problems like pollution and the threat of nuclear disaster".

Anyhow, some educational scientists, like T. Husén, P. Freire, C. Coombs, P. Lengrand, P. Jarvis, e.a. have made explicit efforts to link their discipline to several other disciplines, and to put education within a broad, cultural, social and political perspective. However, it is rather rare to see a pedagogue engage in a discussion, not just with the other behavioral or social sciences, but on top of that, with the natural sciences, especially physics and biology. This has been done very recently by our colleague-comparatist W. Wielemans in a book with the provocative title (our transl.): *Beyond the individual. Images of man in the sciences.* (Wielemans, 1993) His field of study is that of formal (youth) education and educational policy in a comparative perspective. For years, we have been engaged in exchanges and discussions/confrontations on a few areas of common interest: that of the "social dimension" of (adult) education, the concept of "emancipation" and the further development of a comparative science of education. Knowing of my interest for Latin America, he regularly urged me to also look at Asia, and more especially at the Hindu and the Buddhist cultures and countries. With a twist-in-tongue he said: "this may help you to correct your (unit's) orientation on social activism and conscientisation". In the meantime, this "correction" has occurred via the supervision of two doctoral dissertations, one by an Indian scholar from Andhra Pradesh on adult education and people-centred development (Puli, 1987), and one by a Thai supervisor of the Bangkok ministry of Non-Formal Education on community-based learning centres in rural villages (NFE) (Leowarin, 1992). The combination of research and field visits has indeed opened up new perspectives for us, especially a trip to Thailand, land of Buddhist tolerance, gracious hospitality and modernistic pragmatism. The actual NFE-philosophy of "Khit-Pen" propounds the principles of respect, tolerance, unity, and harmony of body and mind and of the eternal bond between man, nature and community. Like in some other countries of Asia and Africa, both the culture and many of its social practices reach indeed "beyond the individual" and reveal a basic tendency to communality.

It is striking to see that the long holistic tradition of such cultures coincides very well with some of the major recent developments - some people even say revolutions - in many of the old and new sciences. Wielemans goes a long way to show that we are experiencing a radical confrontation between an atomistic, individualistic and rationalist view of man and the world on the one hand, and a holistic, integrative and dynamically balanced view on the other. This is the message of post-Newtonian quantum physics stating that matter is a dynamic whole of interrelated particles/waves, of post-Freudian psychology of "relational man" who is at the same time himself-and-many-others, of post-Parsonian sociology stressing the complementarity of individual and collectivity, of post-Darwinist evolution theory. Very revealing, in this respect, is Lovelock's GAIA-hypothesis: "NASA's request to research the possibility of life on the planet Mars lead Lovelock to new questions about life on earth. The result of his very specific approach was 'the development of a hypothesis that the whole scale of living matter on earth, from whales to viruses, and from oak trees to seaweed, might be conceived of as one single living being, which is able to influence the globe in such a way that its need as a totality is being met, and which is gifted with capacities and powers which far surpass those of its composing parts" (Wielemans, o.c, p. 105)

Hence man him/herself has to be seen, not as a monad, but as a "hub of relationships" in an ever evolving world. "Maybe, man is an experiment in free choice and, as such, the greatest venture of Gaia's evolution up to now. Such a hypothesis is fascinating and deeply inspiring. The crisis character of our times thereby evaporates. Instead, we get the feeling of living in a world where we can look upon ourselves as never before" (Wielemans, o.c., p. 108-109)

Looking at this analysis, the aforementioned TV-series, and other publications, one might state that we seem to be moving towards a new era, which some call post- or late-modern. This term contains a reference to the just-terminated period, and is reactive in nature. One could also say that we are entering a new type of Renaissance, which we could call "Econaissance", the birth of a truly ecological view of man and the world.

At the time that we are (were) writing the present introduction, we do not know what implications the author will formulate for the field of pedagogy and education. But it will not fall short of a playdoyer for an integrated, both person- and society-oriented model of education and a school curriculum which will be based on a "gaian view of man and the world", with more integration than separation, less separate subjects and courses and more "basic dimensions", more cooperation than competition, a greater stress on attitudinal and emotional components, and more group and project work than piecemeal individual or classroom work.

Many of us - and most certainly practitioners and theorists of education who have long been working in that direction - will feel confirmed and enriched by such a proposal.

On the other hand, everyday reality is far more in contradiction with this "Gaian" view than we may wish to admit. Wine connoisseurs say that "the truth lies in the glass". Good wine, as we know, contains a strong balance between three of the four basic taste factors: sweetness, bitterness and acidity. Using the wine-metaphor again, we may say that the wine the world is pouring in our glasses these days is excessively sour and bitter. Yes, the Berlin wall has fallen, but instead of "one world block" and a "New World Order", we are confronted with nationalistic, religious and ethnic conflicts and outright wars. Yes, there is a clear rise in ecological consciousness following the action of new social movements, but looking at the yearly reports of the World Watch Institute, the "lesson of Tsjernobil" has not been learned. Yes, there is an ecumenic movement to unite the religions of the world and to promote peace and justice, but when pope John-Paul II brought church leaders together to pray for peace in Assisi, one of them prayed for the "righteous victory" of his followers, and the issue of female priests divides the christian churches. And looking at our own area of education, yes, there is a concept of integrative lifelong learning and "comprehensive education", but the analysis of one of our colleagues at the end of his academic career was that the principles and proposals for "public instruction" formulated by J.M.A. Condorcet in year 2 of the French revolution - that is in 1792 - had nowhere been credibly applied in present day school systems. (De Keyser, 1986)

Has the "gaian hypothesis" already been disconfirmed, even before it was fully worked out? One answer could be similar to that of the Tibetan spiritual leader, the Dalai Lama, coming from his exile to Thailand, in order to join an action in favour of the liberation of another peace Nobel prize Winner, Burmese Aun Sang Sjuu Sjin: "respect for liberty and freedom of all individuals and all ethnic groups in the post-cold war period is the right principle, but we need time and patience for everyone to accept this". Another answer could lie in the direction of some post-modernists: the "gaian hypothesis" is just another of the Great ideological Discourses, and we better do away with it, for there just is not one structuring principle for reality. A third answer, and one we prefer, might be that Gaia is a teleological hypothesis, which can only surmount the contradiction of unity and diversity, of harmony and violence, by means of an extrapolation, based on a specific "reading" of the evolution of man and nature. One of the first scientists to come up with such a teleological hypothesis was Teilhard de Chardin in his book "Le phénomène humain".(Teilhard de Chardin, 1964). According to this scientist-of-several-disciplines, the human being is the last stadium in an evolutionary process which will lead us to "the point Omega" of supreme consciousness and unity. The whole cosmos seems to be subjected to the "law of increasing complexity", whereby "consciousness" or "the inner side of things" is a property of all cosmic matter, but with increasing degrees of intensity.

Such a "reading" of evolutionary reality is, in fact, paradoxical, because reality seems to contradict the principle of unity and harmony as often as it confirms it. Other scientists may and do reach the opposite conclusion, as the precited round table clearly showed. And both sides come up with analytically irrefutable arguments. The ultimate explanation may well lie in what Ernst Bloch has called "Das Prinzip Hoffnung" - the principle of hope. (Bloch, 1959, i, 129 - 203). "Gaia" appears to be a well-founded thesis marked by a perspective of hope for humanity and the world. It can only overcome the paradox of its being contradicted by going down the alphabet

of the future and using its last letter, Ω (Greek omega), as a symbol for its "para-disiacal" solution.

*   *   *

What can we do in the meantime? My own answer would be: to accept or to learn to live with the paradox of plurality, of the co-existence of and the confrontation between several paradigms as "basic models for the understanding of reality". This answer is not simply a theoretical one, but one learnt through sometimes painful experience. With many others, we seem to be trying to give meaning to the experi-ence of the plurality of educational paradigms, as different basic approaches of "how people can/may best be helped to learn". In his presidential address to the 1992 14th Conference of the International Society for the History of Education, M. Depaepe made a thoroughly documented overview of the several approaches and paradigms used in that (sub)field of educational sciences since 1918, especially of the methodo-logical confrontations, which constitutes in itself 'a story full of sound and fury'. His analysis, he said, 'demonstrates that there is not, nor will there ever be, one single true conception on the history of education, so that we shall probably have to learn to live with methodological pluralism' (Depaepe, 1993, p. 3). The basic paradigmatic lesson that I have learned is, equally, that "there is not just one exclusively valid and universally applicable concept of (adult) education". When I set out to try to recon-struct the post-World War II evolution of concepts of (adult) education back in 1985, in order to provide colleague-participants in an international conference on "adult education and the challenges of the 1990s" with an analytical framework, we arrived at a distinction of three successively dominant "paradigms": a socio-technological one linked to the discourse of "planned social change", an emancipatory one linked to the current of "conscientisation", and an emerging socio-communicative one linked to the theory of "communicative action".(Leirman & Kulich, 1987, p. 1 f.) With others, we have each time engaged ourselves in the mainstream of each dominant paradigm, without too many misgivings. However, our analysis, at that time, was of the "linear-progressive" type: we in fact believed that the youngest "communicative" paradigm, given its critical reaction to its predecessors, was, if not the best, at least the temporarily most adequate alternative.

Under the influence of the post-modernity debate, and through discussions with several colleagues at home and abroad, we have had to revise this position. The present book takes on, therefore, the form of a retrospective analysis of what we have experienced as "dominant paradigms" of (adult) education, but this time from the perspective of plurality. One could call it an educational socio-biography. Moreover, we feel inclined to go further back in history, in order to better understand what is happening in the last part of the 20th century. The reading of a just published book about *Adult education and theological interpretations*, to which we made a contribution, really underscores such a perspective (Jarvis, 1992). N. Slee is right when she states, in the concluding chapter, that the book reveals "tensions" and "polar opposites" : individual versus communal, cognitive versus affective, developmental versus conversion perspectives.

To express such a form of plurality, and its many hidden characteristics, I first felt attracted by the metaphor of a "four-face", i. e. a sequence of dominant theoretical and praxis faces with many irrational traits, which, in the final analysis, might well prove to constitute a kind of a quadrant or a four-dimensional reality. The use of the term "four-face" is in itself paradoxical, however, for at least two reasons. First of all, it suggests unity-in-differentiation: each face is different from any other, yet at the same time, they constitute "one family": can both be true? Secondly, the term "face" seems to suggest the individual stance of an "educator" taking on a specific "role" or "position" in relation to his "learners", "participants" or "clients". In that sense, the "face of the educator" would be the basic determinant factor. I therefore switched to the term of "culture" as a set of values, norms and assumptions of a supra-individual nature. Indeed, I want to point at broader entities than individuals, e.g. "schools of thought", "educational institutions" and "global practices", guided by both rational and irrational norms and beliefs. In the context of this book, the term culture has a threefold meaning: a conglomerate of values and norms, a behavioral identity of people, and a social and institutional reality expressing more or less the same cultural contents.

Our reconstructive tale of four cultures - the cultures of expertise, engineering, prophecy and communicative action - will therefore not be restricted to theory or literature alone. Having gone the way from the practice to the theory of education myself, I have always tried to relate the world of thinking to the world of doing. This explains the combination of theoretical analyses with practice-oriented research examples and exemplary practices. And since this is another lesson which I, with many others, have had to learn, I will not confine myself to our origins of "socio-cultural" education, where we tended to view ourselves as "central innovators", but include different sectors and different approaches, from "soft" to "hard", from "school" over "community centre" to "enterprise".

This is not, of course, the first attempt to analyze several paradigms or, better, cultures of (adult) education. I have been especially inspired, first of all, by W. Banning's historical analysis of four influential "types of adult education" (Banning, w., 1959), by Elias and Merriam's six "approaches" to education - from "Liberal" to "Analytical" - (Elias & Merriam, 1980), by Lesne's 4 "modes de travail pédagogique" (Lesne, 1978). I was also inspired by J. A. Stalpers' analysis of "three modes of thinking": regulative, mutational, symbolical. (Stalpers, 1981). More recently, I started to look more at education from an organisational and policy-oriented point of view, coming across analyses like those of Schäfter's six modes of organising educational offerings (Schäfter, 1981), Van der Krogt & Plomp's 4 basic models of training-within-industry (Van der Krogt & Plomp, 1989) and, very recently, the description of "four paths to innovation" by Bouwen & Fry. The latter authors start from the vantage point of "the learning organisation", and distinguish 4 "models of innovation: power model, sales model, expert model and confrontational learning model". (Bouwen & Fry, 1991). This organisational dimension justifies our use of the term culture, since the literature shows that the different paths to innovation each reveal a distinct organisational culture.

Shall we not confuse the reader and ourselves at both a higher and a deeper level? Or positively formulated: will "Gaia" come back at the end of our analysis? We ourselves are not sure, since this introduction was written before we started to write the present book. If the reader is curious, so are we: the end is open.

Walter Leirman
February 1993.

THE EXPERT-CULTURE OF EDUCATION: THE POWER OF KNOWLEDGE LEADS TO POWER OVER LIFE

When H.C. Grattan set out to trace back the history of (adult) education at a world scale, he gave his work the title "The quest for knowledge". (Grattan, 1974). The idea that education makes people overcome their ignorance by true insight, and gain power over life, is indeed a very old one.

Thus, the greek Philosopher Parmenides, writing his poem "Nature" about 500 B.C., depicts his "ascension" to the goddess of truth, in a chart drawn by two horses, and attended by the daughters of the sun. The goddess teaches him about the fundaments of truth and explains the misgivings and misinterpretations of most humans on earth. Through motion and experience, people can be liberated from the sphere of *doxa*, i.e. of mere impressions and shallow opinions, and guided on to the sphere of *alètheia*, i.e. of pure and deep truth. For one who has reached this stadium, such phenomena as changes in physical forms and in human opinion are not in contradiction with the solid fundament of Being, which is one, invariable and immutable. However, this one-ness of being is not reflected in cosmic reality, which is not harmonious at all, since two opposing forces are operating in it: "fire" and "night", i.e. light and darkness. Parmenides did not find an answer to the problems of this opposition. But he had been borne to a temple dedicated to an unnamed goddess, and had experienced the Light of truth. Therefore, he, the poet-philosopher, saw it as his task to transmit it to his fellow humans, and especially to young people, whom he considered to be open and flexible.

There is a clear parallel between the Greek "ascension to truth" and the "revelation of God to mankind" in the great traditional religions: God or a Supreme Being reveals the truth to his prophets Moses, Christ, Mohammed or Buddha, and asks them to become messengers of "the knowledge of good and evil" among his people. And the revelation often happens on a high mountain or a plateau, lit by fire or dazzling white light. According to two "semiologists" of "the world of symbols", the universality of this imagery is striking. Its basic characteristics are the following:

1. The mountain provides a junction between heaven and earth.
2. The holy mountain is situated in the centre of the world.
3. The temple is assimilated to the mountain, and reproduces the cosmic conceptual scheme. (De Champeaux & Sterckx, 1966, p. 164 f.)

22

The clearest illustration of this can be found in the central asian *stupa* or pagoda of Buddha - which is an oriental replica of the etruscan *tumulus*. The most famous example is to be found in Angkor, Cambodia. Originally, this was a round "dome" built on a quadrangular basis, a part of which was hidden under the ground. Thus, heaven, earth and the infernal world were united. Later on, the hemispherical "dome" received a conic upward extension, representing the "axis of the world".

Figure 3: Buddhist Stupa (De Champeaux & Sterckx, 1966)

Building upon the hellenic culture, the Jewish-Christian tradition basically retained this conceptual cosmic scheme, with two major changes: it personified God, and made man into "the master of the world" after he had got to know "the tree of good and evil", i.e. the knowledge of everything. The dualistic image of the human person was, however, maintained by this tradition, and carried right through the so-called dark Middle Ages into the modern times of Enlightenment and Aufklärung. Thus, an antagonism between the "spirit" or the "soul" and the "body" and "all earthen matter" was created, which has survived into the present times. Many of us have experienced it during their own school education in the 1950s and the '60s.

The advent of modern science, from Descartes to Newton and from Leibnitz to Kant, basically meant the de-sacralisation of human knowledge. Human rationality became the supreme value, and God and religion were reduced to "a subject matter for scientific analysis". At first, the scientific academy, and later, the modern university became the institutional expression of this "scientific revolution". Academies and universities were looked upon as "temples of knowledge", and sometimes their buildings translated this message in their architecture. One of the most memorable examples is to be found in Jerusalem, "capital" of three religions and fighting arena of three cultures. Look west, to one of the highest surrounding hills, Mount Scopius, and you'll find there the Hebrew University of Jerusalem, which has become a stronger point of visual attraction than nearby Mount Olive. Some of its buildings indeed have the form of a temple or a dome. To gain knowledge is to climb up a high mountain! Elsewhere in the world, "learned" institutions also use symbols expressing the same message. Thus, one of our colleague universities employs the burning torch in its logo, surrounded by the latin device: "Scientia vincere tenebris" - Defeat darkness through science.

The power of this culture of knowledge-lead education, as well as the changes and vicissitudes it underwent through history, is impressively illustrated in Th. Ballauff's book *Lehrer sein einst und jetzt* (To be a teacher, then and now) (Ballauff, 1985). Informal learning and "natural teaching" e.g. by parents, of course preceded the "professionalisation" of teaching, the first instances of which were the Egyptian "scribents" and their "writing schools" for administrators during the time of the Pharaohs and the "public lectures" of Greek "sophists" on the public markets of the 5th century B.C. According to Ballauff, the first Greek teachers - a curious new type of profession - basically drew upon the Parmenidean, and later, Platonic concept of a *dialogue between teacher and "listeners" leading them onto the autonomy of critical thinking*: 'the original boundedness onto the senses, and the rigidity of fixed perception were given up' in favour of the *Logos*, which people have to discover by themselves (o.c. p. 26). Entering into the world of the Logos, a person becomes liberated, but at the same time responsible at the personal and the societal level: 'a person belonging to the Logos, will be able to speak adequate and evaluating words, especially in the sphere of the community and the state, in the meeting on the public market'. But very soon, this "education towards critical public discourse" was perverted into the "art of rhetoric and fluent speech", and both Socrates and Plato heavily criticised rhetoric and manipulation of the public. But, says a wise Ballauff, teachers had to win the acceptance of their (paying) students, and of the society at large: subsistence comes before philosophy.

Two other traditions which have significantly contributed to our thinking on education, learning and teaching are the judaic tradition of divine wisdom and the christian tradition of mediation of salvation. In such Old Testament books as "Proverbs", "Preacher" and "Jesus Sirah", we are confronted with exhortations to open up oneself to the wisdom of God, as it is imparted by experienced and venerable teachers. Age, both of the tradition and of the teachers, becomes a central argument. We thus read in Jesus Sirah (34 - 35):

Step into the rows of the old
and join their wisdom
Be pleased to hear every speech
and do not miss any wise proverb

In the christian tradition, the basic message is that God has redeemed man from his sinful mortality through his son Jesus. Jesus is the model teacher - in the gospel of John, 60 of the 90 titles applied to Jesus identify him as the teacher. The "disciples" have been taught by him during his public life, and their mission is "to go and BRING THE GOOD MESSAGE TO THE PEOPLE". (Peterson, 1984, p. 6.). Mc Caffry, writing about the "priesthood of the teacher" adds: 'Jesus himself from his Jewish tradition would know the teacher, the rabbi, as a reader, a lawyer, a scholar. It is interesting to see that the teacher, in this sort of context, is considered to be one with authority, not necessarily from themselves but with an empowerment from the tradition. In this sense, the teacher is the interpreter, the translator, the mediator, the converser; the approach is a combination of respect for the content of the teaching, which is hallowed by its origins and development, and respect for the individuality of the recipient. The syllabus is offered to, rather than created by, the learners; but the mode in which the learners operate under that syllabus is Progressive, in that it is not dictated in advance' (Mc Caffry, 1993, p. 56)

Originally, the basic method used for this type of teaching was the "dialogue", a method inherited from the Greek, and especially from Plato. Many syllabuses containing teacher-learner dialogues have been left to us, from "The book of the laws of the countries" by Bardesanes of Edessa in the 1st century A.D. over the "disputationes" or "learned discussions" in scholastic Middle Age to the "discussion books" of the Renaissance. But as Ballauff notes, the dialogue evolved from the 'expression of the struggle for truth' to an instrument for mediating salvation' (o.c. p. 29). Although we cannot repeat or resume his analysis here, we may retain one of its basic conclusions: through (western) history, there is a constant pendular movement between a rich, dialogical and dynamic concept and practice of the teacher-learner relationship centred around the discovery of truth and wisdom, and a reduced, instrumental and static concept and practice centred around the transmission of predetermined contents. Such a movement is highly influenced by the social and political situation, which is at times open and people-centred, and at times closed and authority-centred.

With many others, Ballauff criticises the present situation: 'The present era has subjected itself to the metaphysics of technology, of man as subject and object of creation. We are not moving any longer in the garden of Eden, nor in Gods creation or in familiar relationships... The most simple definition of the teacher is that of the transmitter of knowledge... The teacher is the broker between "the educative goods" and the pupils... Teachers are seen as social engineers, as organizers of learning processes, as multiplicators and informants. Didactics is celebrating its triumphs' (o.c. p. 74)

The reference to the garden of Eden is of special interest here. One of the opening stories of the Genesis book - the tale of the creation of the universe and of man and woman and of their expulsion from paradise - is usually interpreted as the story of the downfall of the human race. In this interpretation, learning is equated with the eating of a forbidden fruit, an act of rebellion against God and the order of Eden. The price to be paid for this sinful act is double: labour "in the sweat of our faces", and conflict between man and woman. Since modern times, the christian churches have accepted the fact that Genesis is not a history book, but a book of symbolic tales illustrating the relationship between God and humankind, man and nature, and man and woman. The explanation offered by traditional church teaching, as we often heard it, is that of a moral lesson: man was not created for the purpose of know-ledge-an-sich but for the purpose of incorporation in the natural and divine order. He was invested with great powers, e.g. he "gave names to all animals", meaning that humankind distinguished itself from animals by giving and expressing meaning through language. Yet, human knowledge, however valuable, must be subjected to ethic principles. Instead of that, humankind separated rationality from morality, with all the consequences we have since learnt to know...

There are, however, quite different interpretations to that story. One is presented by P. Jarvis, following the analysis made by G. von Rad in 1961 (Jarvis, 1993, p. 141 f.). The serpent tempted Eve to eat from the tree of good and evil, telling her: 'For God knows that when you eat of it your eyes will be opened, and you will be like God, knowing good and evil' (Genesis, 3:5) The serpent, which may in fact represent the innate human drive to know and understand, points at the possibility of extending human existence beyond the limits set by God at creation. The serpent seems to ask WHY NOT? 'Why should humankind not know more, if there is more to be known? Why should individuals not develop beyond limits imposed externally? Why should not humankind reach out and become as gods? ' (o.c. p. 146)

There are two other implications of this famous story. One is pointed out by Jarvis when he interprets the well known verse: "And they knew that they were naked". According to him it means 'they knew that they had learned.. Learning, then, lies at the very essence of humanity; learning is at the heart of growth. Here humankind is different from the animal kingdom - animals can be taught, as the behaviourists have shown - but can they inquire and learn without being taught?. ... Learning lies beyond education and at the centre of human experience itself. Learning is the process of transforming that experience into knowledge, skills, attitudes and so on... It is, however, not merely a matter of internalizing perceptions of that outside world, it is a matter of experiencing it - either through direct action or through language - and then reasoning and thinking about it and thereafter reaching an understanding of it.' (o.c. p. 147) To this deep and meaningful commentary, we might add that the story also tells us that human learning, seen as transformation of experience into "knowledge", is a process fraught with labour and pain, because it means leaving "paradise" or "established order" for the hard world of new insights and opinions.

A second implication still has to do with the finding that one is "naked". Traditional paintings of the scene, showing indeed Adam and Eve looking in shame at each other's near-nakedness bear sexual overtones, or at least suggest the meaninglessness of the (sinful) body before the power of the divine spirit. But, like in some dreams, being naked often means being separated from all others, being thrown back upon oneself. In Jungian terms, one might say that this is about the archetype of autono-mous rational man. True learning means individuation and separation. In a broader and deeper sense, human existence "after the fall", i.e. after the genesis of human culture, is separation. This is one of the basic statements in the philosophy of E.

Levinas, especially in his works "Totalité et Infini" and "Humanisme de l'autre homme" (Levinas, 1970, 1972). Humankind has learned the lesson of separation and autonomy, to the point of becoming a living protest against every possible totalization or fixed order. In this sense, man is not "like god", but, in the words of a 19th century Dutch poet, "a God in the deepest of his thoughts", or, in the terms of the imagery used above, a temple on the mountain of Selfhood, the master and expert of his own life. The biblical story also says that "man and woman" were not only punished with labour-in-exile, but also with "enmity" between them and between peoples in general. Some have interpreted this as if God sent people to war against one another. But this may symbolise another aspect of separation. In the eyes of Levinas, personhood includes an unquestioned feeling of self-sufficiency and totality, which is exclusive of all other people. The human person is therefore inclined to violence. Fratricide, wars, totalitarian regimes and concentration camps are extreme witnesses to that - even though Levinas prefers to remain within the (inter)personal sphere. Would the "fall" then be a fall into radical autonomy and subjectivism, without any regard for all others and for nature? "Est-ce que je ne tue pas par exister? - do I not kill by existing?" Levinas asks. His answer, and that of other ethically inspired thinkers, will be that the confrontation with the other (written *autre* or *other*) constitutes a radical questioning of the individual's subjectivity and autonomy, and opens up the perspective of solidarity. We will come back to this line of thought in our fourth chapter.

For the time being, there emerges a possibly surprising but clear connection: the oldest concept of education - that of guiding people to the Logos, to truth, wisdom and salvation - seems to coincide with the first learning experience of humankind: that of "eating from the tree of knowledge", and thus becoming an autonomous individual through independent critical thought. The basic tool for such an operation was and is language, for man "gives names to all animals". This scant reference to language is full of meaning, since it does not present language as an existing system of words and sentences, but as a *basic human act*. It is only since the advent of linguistics, and especially the clarification of linguistic structures by De Saussure, that the full implication of the linguistic nature of humankind has started to become part of our cultural consciousness.

However, the ancient Greek, as we learn from the writings of their prominent philosophers, were already aware of the specificity of human language in comparison to the "language of the animals": animal language is fixed and instinct-lead, whereas human language is about meaning and judgment, is basically reflexive. Modern analysts, looking at the Greek discourse of the human gift of Logos, point out that, however dynamic the human speech act may be, ancient Greece situates it within the premises of a fixed Order: Ideas and concepts, the laws of nature, the principles of art and drama, the structure of the ideal state - they all can be discovered, and even made the subject of unending dialogue - but they cannot be altered, let alone "created".

As we already pointed out in our introduction, modern man rejects the idea of a fixed order, and makes truth dependent upon scientific experimentation and/or reflection.

Such an "intellectual act" leads to theories as temporary constructions, which will be subjected to further testing. This modern attitude has engendered miraculous results - the consumer's paradise - and created great problems as well - the social and ecological disorder.

Fixed order or not: ancient Greece and modern times are linked by a radical preference for Logos and rational order. The expert culture of education and learning is basically situated within this classico-modern perspective. Its world view is that of *homo sapiens* i.e. reflective man, and of *enlightened society*. The key issue is the basic ignorance of man and the uninformedness of society. The mission of education is to make people knowledgeable and critical: reflexive citizens will form the basis of a critical society. The oldest and most global definition of learning describes it as "a more or less permanent change in behaviour as a result of experience". This definition is narrowed here to the areas of *cognition and problem-solving*. This is the ability to perceive, distinguish and understand different phenomena in time and space, in and by themselves and in their mutual relationship, and to ask questions and solve problems concerning them. This whole domain of learning has been "mapped" and ordered into a "taxonomy" by B.S. Bloom. He introduced a scale of six goal areas, from rather simple and easy to more complex and difficult: knowledge of facts, understanding reality and its principles, applying these, analyzing and explaining, synthesising, and, finally, evaluating. (Bloom, 1956). Even though there has not been found much empirical evidence for this classification (De Corte e.a. 1978) it reveals at least the vast complexity and varying intensity of the whole cognitive domain.

The strategy most commonly used in the expert culture of education is the so-called *rational-empirical strategy*. It stresses the search for knowledge in continuous confrontation with empirical reality. One well-known example for this is the *Research, Development, Diffusion and Adoption* model, which indicates the basic steps to be taken in order to reach the goal of knowledge acquisition and application. Within this perspective, the educator takes the position of expert and informant. His power base is clearly his expertise: he represents the "authority of knowledge" which learners have to accept. Learners take on the position of information processors and problem-solvers. In the terms of Kolb's learner typology, which will be presented further on, they are seen as "thinkers" more than "doers".

In the expert culture of education, much attention is paid to goals and to their operationalisation, as it was promoted almost to an atomistic level by e.g. Mager & Mager (Mager e.a., 1974): what do we expect the learner to know and to be able to do as a result of his learning experience ? That is the starting point for the "teaching-learning process" and the science of didactics or "didaxology" (Decorte e.a., 1988). Let us look at one of the "models" of that process, that of Van Gelder, which is based on the analyses of the teaching process by Gage and Bruner. His 'model of didactic analysis' is visualised in the picture below. The didactic process contains a sequential whole of four basic components: determining the objectives, diagnosing the initial situation of the learners, constructing a teaching-learning situation with contents, choice of methods, of learning activities and of instruments and materials,

28

and, finally, the determination or evaluation of the results. In a learning kit developed from this model, the future teacher is confronted with 4 key questions: (1) What do I want to reach? (goal) (2) Where do I start from? (initial situation), (3) How can I provide instruction? (teaching-learning situation) and (4) What was the result of my teaching? (evaluation).

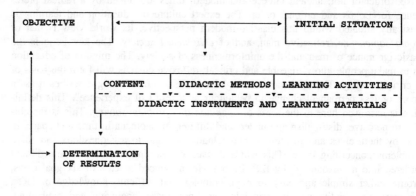

Figure 4: Van Gelder's Didactic Model

These and other models certainly have their merits - many of us have been "trained" as teachers without having any elaborated models at our disposal. It is interesting to look more closely at the teacher's position, however: s/he determines or selects the objectives, plans the process and evaluates it. Results are tested against objectives, and the do-loop of the process ends there. Contextual elements are virtually left out. Inside the process, the "learner" is represented only as an "element of the initial situation" and "executor of learning activities". Furthermore, too little distinction is made between teaching and learning.

The developments in educational c.q. instructional psychology of the past 15 years have clearly modified this kind of "didaxology". According to J. Lowyck, a "cognitive vision on learning" originated, which states that knowledge and skills are learned by way of mental information processing: new information is actively integrated in the existing knowledge base of the learner. (Lowyck, 1992, p.84). Popularly stated: the learner "re-orders his head". We regroup the characteristics of learning given by Lowyck into four basic categories:

(1) *Learning is diagnostic action*: the learner, as main author of the learning process, actively compares his/her previous knowledge of 'what' and 'how' with the new information being offered, and links new insights and skills to older ones;

(2) *learning is goal-oriented*: the object of learning is a well-defined set of new information elements, and from there on, the learner selects the relevant related contents in his memory, stores the new contents in a new place in memory and/or reorders the existing knowledge structure;

(3) *learning is cumulative construction*: humans gradually develop complex networks of knowledge, and new learning contents are 'built into' theses networks; the more we know and can do already, the easier it will be to integrate new knowledge and skills;

(4) *learning is contextual*: new information learned is always related to the personal, social and physical context in which learning takes place; a 'transfer' of information learned to new situations requires an insight into this context.

Let us illustrate these characteristics with a concrete example of a car firm which has run into trouble and lays off 5000 of its workers. Among them a number of secretaries who have been working there for more than ten years. One of these applies for a job in a consultancy firm, and is told she will be hired on the condition that she learns the word-processing computer programme "Word Perfect, version 5.1" as soon as possible. She had been using "MS-WORD 5.0" for 3 years, so she thinks this will be easy. Yet she discovers that she was only partly right. After a one-hour conversation with a course-manager, she takes "a quick course" of 5 evening sessions for "people having basic knowledge of PC-MSDOS and of the principles of word-processing". She quickly discovers that the "Functions" of MS-WORD do not coincide with those of WP, and that the teacher uses another system of presentation of the whole set of functions than the one she learned before (context!). The initial disappointment disappears, when she discovers that, on the whole, the "new" functions are not new at all, but barely ordered differently (diagnostic action). Since her new boss has told her that she will mainly have to "write letters", to adapt and use the "mailing lists" and to make some "tables", she orients her main attention to the related parts of the course (goal-orientation). But how do you efficiently save all these data ? She had developed her own double system of alphabetic and functional classification of the same document, and after presenting this problem to the teacher, she finds an adaptation of her system in the new programme (cumulative construction).

The example given here is taken from our experience. How can we be sure that the real learning experience and its results were those communicated to us by a secretary? The obvious answer is: through research. As we know, research is a container concept with many greatly different methodologies. Traditionally, the expert culture has been connected with the so-called "empirical-analytical" research methodology. For a long time, the basic educational question to be answered was that of the *degree of efficiency of the teaching/learning process*: has the new content/skill been learned indeed? Therefore, the first method used was that of "testing the black-box": learners were tested before and after, or sometimes even only after their "submission to the treatment". In case of a "significant increase in knowledge or skill in the learners", one then concluded that the "treatment" had been successful. If not, the "treatment conditions" had to be changed. One soon discovered, however, that "rival hypotheses" could equally well explain success, such as "other external influences", "normal maturation of the person", "previous sympathy or dislike of the content", "the educative environment" etc. Therefore, several sophisticated designs for "experiments" and "quasi-experiments" were developed, as e.g. in Gage's first handbook on Educational Research (Gage, 1964). We will illustrate one such design in our next chapter. The problem with those designs is indeed the "black-box": whatever the results may be, they do not tell us anything about *the learning process* and *its meaning to learners and teachers.*

The pre-cited cognitive vision on learning has generated a wave of very different research projects. A colleague, specialist in the teaching and learning of mathematics in grammar school, recently introduced us to one outstanding example: the system of what is called *Cognitively Guided Instruction* (Cgi), developed by a group of researchers in the USA (Carpenter & Fennema, 1992; Fennema, Carpenter & Franke, 1993). In an ongoing project which started in 1987, the research team first studied the different strategies children use to solve problems of addition and subtraction. One of the major findings was that children, even before teachers start to offer them formal notions of computation, are already able to solve a number of problems by actions of joining objects together, separating them, putting them into groups, etc. This knowledge is congruent with the experience of adult literacy teachers working, since 1950, with adults who never went to school, as reported e.g. by Unesco. The Wisconsin colleagues were able to develop a taxonomy of problem types in basic mathematics.

The table below offers six problems of addition, subtraction, division and multiplication for first-graders. The difference between them is based on the "typical" strategies children use in solving them, and on the variation of the unknown. Initially, children (and adults?) use a direct and concrete model for their solution by using counters to represent objects: 12 stamps make a set of 12 counters, 8 stamps a set of 8 counters. The simplest operation is "to take 8 away from the pile of 12, so there's 4 left". The situation changes when we have to do with two piles, as in the fourth problem. Children often solve the problem by matching the set or pile of 12 with that of 8, which leads to the conclusion that "12 is 4 more than 8". The fifth problem - division of 12 by 4 -is first solved by ordering 12 counters into groups of 4 and by counting the number of groups. This is in fact a grouping operation ("let's see how many groups of 4 i can make"). The sixth problem is solved by first partitioning 12 counters into 4 equal groups, and then counting the number of objects in each group.

The most difficult problem is the third one, because we start with the unknown: "some stamps". The simplest solution is to "count on" from 8 to 12. However, research on "children in learning action, explaining what they are doing" has revealed that several strategies are being used to rightly solve the same problem! To begin with, there are "concretist" strategies (like counting on your fingers) and "abstract" strategies (using a mental representation). Furthermore, there are different starting positions (e.g. in deducing 37 from 43, you can begin with the lowest or with the highest number), and, connected to that, one can "count on", "count down", "compare", "join", or combine several of these operations.

Table 1: Problems of addition, subtraction, division and multiplication in Cognitively Guided Instruction

1 Sybil had 12 stamps. She gave 8 of them to George. How many stamps did Sybil have left?

2 Sybil had 8 stamps. George gave her some more and then she had 12. How many stamps did George give her?

3 Sybil had some stamps. George gave her 8 more and then she had 12 stamps. How many stamps did Sybil have before George gave her any?

4 Sybil had 12 stamps. George had 8 stamps. How many more did Sybil have than George?

5 Sybil had 12 stamps. She put 4 of the stamps on each page of a book. On how many pages will she put stamps?

6 Sybil had 12 stamps. She wants to divide them so that she and 3 friends have the same number of stamps. How many will each person get?

Are all these differences known to teachers? To find an answer, the researchers did a "baseline study", and found that teachers were able to identify many of the problem types and solving strategies, but that their knowledge was not organised into a coherent system. They also found two types of "beliefs" about teaching: a belief that instruction means one-way transmission of knowledge versus a belief that the role of the teacher is to help students construct mathematical knowledge on the basis of what they already know. One teacher expressed the first type of belief as follows: "It's a big role. I have taught first graders that when they first came in, they didn't have any concept of what adding was... The teacher has to do it step-by-step". Another teacher made a quite contrary statement: "The teacher also has to be the learner. She has to pay attention to where the kids are, learn from them where they are, and dictate what her next step is because there are a lot of different learners and learner's styles..."

CGI basically is in the line of the last quotation: teaching is problem-solving, based on previous knowledge, and allowing for different strategies. This basic assumption was tested out in an experiment whereby 40 teachers were randomly divided over an experimental group of 20, participating in a 4-week summer workshop, and a control group which received no special training. The results, observed during the following school year, were convincing: 'When compared to non-CGI-teachers, CGI-teachers assess their children's knowledge more often and use a larger variety of procedures to gain knowledge about children. Much assessment is integrated into ongoing instruction, when the teachers gain knowledge of children by asking questions and listening to their children's responses.' At the same time, researchers report, mathematics becomes more fun.

This experiment was followed by a case study of six teachers who had participated in the workshop, in order to better understand the changes in their teaching and in the learning of the children. In their conclusion, the authors tackle the question of generalising their results to other age groups and to other subjects with prudence, and end their report as follows: 'our research to date suggests that giving teachers access to research-based knowledge about students' thinking and problem solving can affect profoundly teachers' beliefs about learning and instruction, their classroom practices, their knowledge about their students, and most important, their students' learning and beliefs'.

This interesting piece of research-linked-to-practice bears clear testimony to the cognitive vision on learning and its four characteristics spelled out above, especially the diagnostic and constructivist aspects. Moreover, it combines several methods of research, related to the type of questions being asked, and the same applies to the variety of teaching methods being used. However, one should also look at what is left out from the very "positive" report. The report we read makes reference only once to errors being made, and then by way of negation: 'In individual or small group work, the teachers also asked students to explain their work rather than showing what they did wrong'. All illustrations given are positive ones. Don't students make mistakes, sometimes even repeatedly? Will correction come from explanations among students? Furthermore, the CGI-method relies heavily on verbalisation: what about students who are less gifted in verbal language? And do we have to believe the repeated statement that 'teachers develop their own materials'?

It is possible that other, more extensive reports, contain answers to these questions. Our final remark has to do with the expert culture: cognitively guided instruction, however open, dynamic and creative, is generally operating within the framework of an established "body of knowledge", which is represented by the teacher(s) and the handbooks or materials-in-use. In initial maths teaching, which is about computation, the learners do dispose of their own experiential knowledge, so the teacher appears as one who re-translates and formalises. When things become more abstract and complex, like in geometry, both positions change: the learner moves to mental modelling, and the teacher becomes a "true expert". Mathematics seems to be the expert domain par excellence!

From what precedes, one might conclude that the expert culture is institutionally anchored in schools, from Kindergarten to the Open University, or in training centres. But when one looks around, one encounters other expert systems trying to cognitively guide present and future "client-learners". In their study of more than 4000 examples of "dissemination and utilization of scientific knowledge", R. Havelock e.a.

discovered three "models": the "Problem-Solver Model", the "Social Interaction Model" and the "Research, Development and Diffusion Model" (Havelock, e.a., 1969). The latter one, whereby Research into new problem areas precedes the Development of solution-to-precise-problem packages and their Diffusion amongst as many potential users as possible, may be the best known, even though it does not find too many applications nowadays. Authors like Guba and Clark applied this model in a modified form to the area of school innovation or reform, by adding a 4th phase: Adoption (Guba & Clark, 1968). But even that adaptation has been rejected as too cognitivistic by well-known researchers in the area of school innovation (Vandenberge & Vandenberg, 1986).

One model which has been in regular use since the beginning of the 1960s, both in research and in practice, is the "Social Interaction Model", which has been renamed into "Diffusion of Innovations" c.q. "Innovation-Decision" by two rural sociologists, E. Rogers and R. Shoemaker (Rogers, 1962, Rogers & Shoemaker, 1971). The basic focus is on the decision-making process in persons who are being confronted with innovations. The term innovation covers a whole range of offerings: new ideas, new procedures, new products, new models of action, etc. Two practical examples are marketing offensives for new products and campaigns by authorities to divulge new measures or to prevent the spread of illnesses like Aids. The central point of attention in this model is the individual adoption process, which starts on the moment that a potential user takes up information about the innovation, and ends with the decision to adopt or reject it, on the basis of an evaluation.
In their first analysis of ca 400 specific cases in different areas of practice (agriculture, industry, education, medicine), Rogers e.a. originally came to the conclusion that persons adopting an innovation went through five consecutive phases:

(1) *awareness* of the new idea, product, etc.
(2) *interest* into the innovation and further information-seeking
(3) mental *evaluation* of its usefulness
(4) *trial* of the innovation on a small scale, using new information
(5) *adoption* conditioned by positive experience in the trial phase

Continued research in diverse practice fields, mostly in the form of post-hoc in-depth interviews with persons having adopted or rejected an innovation, lead to the finding that the adoption process contained phases or stadia indeed, but the initial 5-phase theory needed some revision: the so-called adoption-process sometimes ends in rejection, the duration of the process varies from person to person, some "phases", like the "trial" phase, are skipped because of lack of time or opportunities to test and evaluate, and phases do not always follow the indicated sequential pattern.

In accordance with these findings, Rogers e.a. modified their 5-phase model on a number of points. Instead of "adoption process", they now used the term "innovation-decision process" as 'the mental process through which an individual passes from first knowledge of an innovation to adoption or rejection and to later confirmation of this decision' (o.c. p. 26). They no longer talked about phases but about "functions" i.e. operations needed to successfully conclude the process, they added the important "confirmation" function, paid more attention to antecedent and process variables, and distinguished between first and final adoption/rejection.

The whole theory is visualised in the figure on the following page. We will briefly explain it, and then offer a research example from the field of general adult education. According to Rogers' findings, an innovation process starts with the *knowledge* function. However, taking real notice of a new idea, depends on so-called *antecedent variables*, which are grouped into three categories: personality characteristics, social characteristics and the perceived need for the innovation. The first group contains such aspects as the degree of intelligence, the general attitude towards change and innovation, the level of education: the higher or more positive they are, the greater the probability that persons will show active interest in an innovation. In the second category, we find variables like the degree of integration in a social system, "cosmopoliteness" or the openness to renewal, the value attached to specific innovations: here again, the better or more positive these are, the higher the correlation with the knowledge function. That there has to be a "perceived need for the innovation" looks self-evident, and so too the finding that, under certain conditions, needs can be provoked or even manipulated by the way the "change agents" present the innovation.

Right from the beginning of an innovation-decision process, the social system exerts its undeniable influence: are the norms prevailing in the system congruent with those of the innovation (think of promotion campaigns for condom use), is there a high or a low degree of tolerance for "deviant" ideas and actions (think of civil disobedience campaigns), is the system in itself well-integrated or is it highly fragmented, etc.?

What was called "awareness" before, is now called "knowledge". For Rogers e.a. this may mean three things:

- being informed that there is an innovation and having a vague notion of its nature;
- how-to-knowledge of the innovation itself (where to get it, how to use it etc.)
- knowledge of the basic principles of the innovation.

The latter form, which we might call "knowledge why", is not in fact necessary for a person in order to adopt an innovation, but it may be useful for the evaluation of this or later innovations. It is important to note that the authors did not find a direct correlation between the degree of knowledge and the degree of adoption of an innovation. With the *persuasion* function, we move almost naturally to the sphere of personal and social attitudes in its two basic dimensions of sympathy/antipathy and inclination to action. At a certain moment, the individual starts to "make up his mind" and generates a general opinion about the innovation, using different kinds of information. An aspect of this process is a "mental trial" or evaluation: when this is feasible, the individual will reach the decision stage sooner. Should s/he hesitate,

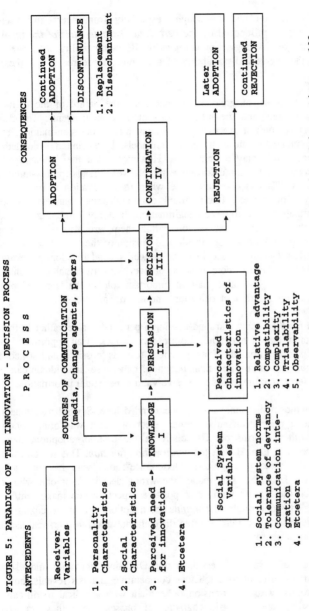

FIGURE 5: PARADIGM OF THE INNOVATION - DECISION PROCESS

slightly adapted from: ROGERS, E. & SHOEMAKER, F. (1971) *Communication of innovations*, p.102

then new information will be sought, especially from peers and friends. This evaluation is highly influenced by the *perceived characteristics of the innovation*: its relative advantage, its degree of complexity, its compatibility with one's personal convictions, the   perceived possibility of a try-out, the degree of complexity of the innovation.

Two other factors are of great importance here: the nature of the communication channels being used, and the interventions of a "change agent". The diffusion of innovations is not only a process of individual mental decision-making, but also of constant communication through various channels. In the initial "knowledge" stage, the mass media will play a great role. However, from the "persuasion" moment onwards, interpersonal communication with relatives, friends, professional peers etc. becomes crucial. This is especially true when the innovation is more "ideal" than "technical" or "pragmatic". Interpersonal communication channels do not simply provide information, but above all legitimation. It is not surprising that social networks, and the location of the person within them, are also of great importance: people with many relations, both inside and outside of their usual social system, and occupying a fairly central place in these networks, tend to adopt innovations more easily than those who are more isolated or occupying marginal positions. Interventions of a "change agent" also play an important role in the "middle" phase. They often consist of information, clarification, and emotional support.

The *decision function* centres around making a personal choice, either in the direction of adoption or in that of rejection. The presence or lack of an opportunity to perform a real trial is often crucial. If a "practical test" is possible and asked for, then adoption occurs far more often than rejection. Otherwise, individuals can again call upon their interpersonal relations to receive valid experiential information.

In the former model, the innovation process ended here. Several researchers showed, however, that a prior decision to either reject or adopt was often followed by a search for further information. Especially in the case of adoption, persons were looking for confirmation. Hence, the *confirmation function*. This search for additional information may lead to cognitive "dissonance": one who has just adopted the innovation now finds that s/he made "the wrong decision", or one who rejected it now finds that there are a number of positive aspects which make him/her deplore the decision. Thus one might *discontinue* the adoption, or, on the contrary, arrive at *later adoption*. Such a "switch" is often difficult, however, for personal as well as for social or financial reasons.

At first glance, this "second" version of the Diffusion-Innovation model looks very different from its original parent. Close comparative analysis reveals, however, that we are confronted with an extension rather than with a radical modification. Thus, "functions" still have the basic character of phases, since they are sequentially ordered in time, and there is a clear analogy between former phases and new functions :

"awareness" = "knowledge",
"interest + mental evaluation" = "persuasion",
"trial + adoption" = "decision-making".

"Confirmation" is in fact the only newcomer on the innovation process scene. The most important additions are the "antecedent" and "process variables", which give the model the character of a combined individual and social innovation process theory. Close attention to the inter-individual differences in the rate and speed of adoption further allowed the authors to distinguish five kinds of adopters: *innovators, early adopters, early majority, late majority and laggards.*

A more important question may be: on what grounds do we situate this model within our expert culture? The great stress on communication and interaction seems to indicate that we better locate it elsewhere, e.g. in the engineering or in the communicative culture. Some may even conclude that the model has nothing to do with education.

There can be little doubt that the innovation-decision model is of a mixed nature. Personally, I prefer to locate it primarily within the expert culture for the following reasons: two of the four functions are cognitive in nature (knowledge and decision-making), the whole process is one where new information is continually gathered and worked through, learning, and especially cognitive learning, is at the heart of the process, and the so-called "change agent" assumes the position of informant and consultant.

Let us now look at a research example. It is part of a huge 5-year project, in which a social-cultural voluntary organisation - the K.A.V. or League of Christian Workers' Women - cooperated with two research centres of our university: Applied Social Psychology and Social Pedagogy or adult continuing education. The details of this so-called P.O.M.-project are spelled out in our next chapter. Suffice it to note here that the basic issue was *educational opportunities for working class girls* , and that the project was divided into two phases: a "social-psychological" phase of research into the attitudes of a representative group of 2560 female members spread over 25 local sections, and a "social-pedagogical" phase of information, sensibilisation and action. The project started in 1968 and ended in 1973. In the second phase, we made a random selection of 15 local sections - called A-sections - with whom we would set up an action-oriented research project around three basic goals:

- diffusion of information about secondary education for girls and of the data about members' attitudes ; ("knowledge goal")

- promotion of personally justified attitudes towards the central issue ; ("attitudinal goal")

- promotion of participation of representatives from the working class in local school policy making ("action goal").

Table 2: A Process scale for testing the diffusion of innovation among KAV-members in the project "educational opportunities for working class girls" (P.O.M.)

PHASE – CONTENT LEVEL	AWARE-NESS	INTE-REST	EVALU-ATION	TRIAL	ADOP-TION
1. GENERAL NOTION OF THE PROJECT					
2. A PROJECT WITHIN KAV					
3. GENERAL AND SPECIFIC GOALS OF THE PROJECT	At KAV-meetings, I've heard about the goals of the project	I would like to read more about the goals of P.O.M.	I've been thinking about local problems of education for girls	I've been discussing the specific aims of the project with others	I can tell you what we will try to reach here in our section
4. RESEARCH ACTIVITIES AND RESULTS					
5. EXCHANGE OF OPINION ABOUT EDUCATION FOR GIRLS					
6. EXPRESSING ONE'S OWN OPINION					
7. ACTION WITH KAV AROUND PARENTS' PARTICIPATION					
8. ACTIVE INDIVIDUAL PARTICIPATION IN THE PROGRAMME					
9. EXTERNAL ACTION WITH KAV					

These goals and their contents were definitely new to the KAV-movement. As researchers, we were interested i.a. in knowing to which degree these goals would be realised. One of the ways to do that was the application of Rogers' diffusion model to the three-year action project at the level of local members. To that purpose, we used Lazarsfeld's "panel-technique", whereby a group of 300 local members would be interviewed on three moments: somewhere in the middle of the action project (fall '72), at its immediate end (fall '73) and about one year after its termination (summer '74). In the line of the empirical-analytical tradition, a set of 17 hypotheses were formulated, grouped around 4 categories: the speed and intensity of adoption, the influence of several media, the influence of different levels of participation in the KAV, and the degree of personal involvement of members in the issue and the programming activities surrounding it. (Vandemeulebroecke, 1977)

The main instrument used in this research was based on Rogers' original 5-phase theory, since the "new" version was not yet available at the time of preparation. In the case of the KAV-project, we could not talk about one "single innovation" - as the three main goals spelled out above prove. Moreover, the innovation was much more "ideal" than "practical". For these reasons, great attention was paid to the preparation of the instrument. We decided to distinguish 9 consecutive levels of intensity of realisation within each phase, from easier KNOWING (1-4), over FEELING (5-6) to difficult ACTING (7-9). We constructed a set of 5 x 9 concrete behaviours of members, each of them expressing one phase and one level of intensity. We used a group of 20 "judges", all of them professionals or leaders within the movement, having a solid knowledge of the project as a whole, and of the research data of the 1st phase in particular. This lead to a considerable amount of remarks and we had to rework half of our items. One interesting feature was that, for 3 of the 9 intensity levels, the judges put our "adoption" items in Phase III and "evaluation" and "trial" items in Phase IV and V. When confronted with these data, some of them explained: "in our movement, it is like this: people first do something, and then they start thinking about it...". The new scale was submitted again to our judges, and this time we obtained a very good fit between our scheme and their judgment. The next table shows the combination of 9 levels and 5 phases, and contains the five specific items for level 3, "GENERAL AND SPECIFIC PROJECT GOALS". Interviews were held at the members' homes in a private conversation between the researcher and the member. After the initial identification questions, the interviewer presented the concrete statements in 5 stacks of 9 cards each, asking the interviewee to lay aside those items which she thought "applied to herself". For each of the items thus retained, an additional validating question was asked to see whether the interviewee could "illustrate" or "give more details about" the item.

Of the many results presented in the final report, we only retain one: the percentage of the panel reaching a specific dimension, at the three interview moments, i.e. in 1972, 1973 and 1974. Our figure on the next page depicts these results.

Before discussing results, a remark needs to be made: the phases I & II (Awareness/interest) and IV-V (Trial/adoption) were taken together, because nearly all

40

persons reaching phases I or IV also reached the next phases II or V. This regrouping can also be interpreted as a kind of post-facto validation of Rogers' second model, taking into account the "broad" interpretation of the knowledge function. Globally, we find little evolution or "growth" from one year to another. Moreover, there is a fairly equal distribution over three stadia in the process: about 1/3 remains unaffected by the project, nearly 1/3 reaches the stage of Awareness, and about 1/4 reaches the final stages of Trial/Adoption. About 1/10 occupies the middle position of Evaluation. This seems to confirm the statement of our "judges" that members easily move from "interest" to "action", but do not "think so much", at least not immediately. Looking at the data per year, we see that there is a clear backdrop after one year. One reason for this may well be the time of the interviews: they were realised at the end of the 1972 summer holidays, or just around the start of a new programme in September-October. At that time, the movement is quasi inactive. A more finely

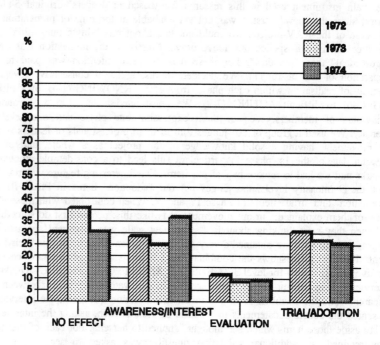

Figure 6: Percentage of members reaching a given phase over three years in the P.O.M.-project

tuned analysis of the proportion of positive answers for each of the 45 items over the three years - an analysis which we cannot reproduce here because of its exten-siveness - lead to a more nuanced conclusion: there was a systematic and significant positive change for *Evaluation* and *Trial* as a whole, and for a part of the *Interest* items. There was no such change for Awareness and Adoption.

In evaluating these results, one has to look, of course, at the complex and "ideal" nature of the innovation. Rogers' repeated remark that many innovations, even those of a rather technical or pragmatic nature, sometimes take 4 to 8 years before any fair degree of adoption is reached, should be borne in mind here. Moreover, an idea like "working class girls - or even girls in general - should receive an opportunity to do further studies" was far less generally accepted as a social norm back in 1972 than it is in 1993!

The whole set of results of the project allowed the main researcher to construct a theory of general adult education within voluntary organisations, along the lines of Rogers' first and second model (Vandemeulebroecke, o.c., p. 411 f.). One of its central propositions states: a general education movement is globally capable of diffusing information and promoting problem-analysis and sensibilisation among its members, but is not capable of directly provoking adoption or application of new insights and attitudes. At best, it can support and structure the adoption process, so that members are better able to take justified decisions and act consequently.

In retrospect, one may ask questions about the nature of the instrument, containing items which presented interviewees with fairly behaviouristic translations of project goals and contents. That was in accordance, however, with the prevailing research paradigm of those days. Another question concerns the positioning of the project as a common enterprise of the whole movement, regardless of local differences in membership, programming and school situation. The central organisation acted here, in fact, as the expert-innovator, making an offer to the local groups. That is entirely consistent with the "diffusion of innovations" - model. Part of that offer consisted, however, of their own answers to questions about "further education for girls", so that one can plead that there was a certain "perceived need", at least in that area of the project. Furthermore, each local section was fed back its own results, which they could freely discuss.

Finally, one may remark that, by considering the educator-counsellor of local sections as a "communication channel" and a "process variable", one does not get a true picture of the educative relationship. A clear result of the project was that it challenged leaders and educators of the organisation in their rather optimistic beliefs about "education towards action", and provided them with a more realistic view on the limited, but real possibilities of their work.

Since the 1980s, innovation has become a central point of attention in the world of professional for-profit organisations, and in the related study fields of psychology and sociology of organisations. Two specialists in both practice and research on organisational innovation and learning start their review of 13 case studies with the following statement: 'Probably never before in human history have so many businesses and social organisations had to cope with so many fundamental changes at such an increasing rate of change. External pressures in the economic and political environment as well as internal pressures of new technologies and the changing attitudes of members, threaten the survival of these organisations' (Bouwen & Fry, 1991, p. 37). In defining innovation as 'development and implementation of new ideas by people who over time engage in transactions with others within an institutional order', they focus not on individual innovation-decisions, but on the interaction among people in an organisational context. Their main question is: what has the organisation learned from the innovation effort, and how did this happen? Or in other terms: how did the organisation move from "the old logic" to the "new logic"?

The analysis of their extensive case materials leads them to the discovery of four "pathways" or "models", as was already indicated in the introduction. One of these is called "the expert model": for the realisation of a desired innovation, the organisation designates one or more experts, who will initiate a problem-solving process and follow a rational step-by-step procedure involving as many participants as possible, in order to arrive at a common solution based on well-argumented insights. They illustrate the model with a practical case, which we will relate here with only minor alterations.

We find ourselves in a medium-sized company renamed here COMMUNICATIONS. It is a highly specialised firm, with a strong functional hierarchy and a strong concern for quality. Its products are well known, and highly innovative by market standards. International developments force them to reconsider the introduction of a new CAD/CAM (Computer Assisted Design c.q. Manufacturing) system in the department of design and development. This new system will shorten the time needed for planning and production. They made an internal effort in this direction five years before, but without success. This time they hire a special project manager.

From the start, the manager proclaimed and followed a principle of twofold integration: all related functions have to be included, and all levels - from designers to the director - have to be involved. He described his approach as follows:

"We always initiate a first proposal. This proposal is explained to the designers. For example, my proposal was to use a 200 dots electrostat for the drawing table. We had been showing examples and the different options and asked them: "Look, these are the alternatives and these are the possibilities of the system. What is most appropriate now in your situation?
If you just ask for alternatives, you don't get an answer. They don't understand anything, you have to explain this to them. After the explanation we considered all options, they had a say in it and they dropped the 200 dots proposal very quickly after I gave them the proper information."

From then on, there started a communication process which can be characterised as oriented to the problem at stake and linear. Project-group meetings were held, which roughly followed the same pattern: problem definition, clarification, proposing alternatives, evaluation, decision. There was a continuous involvement of most users, and one could even notice an eagerness to start among the designers. The project leader made a final 250-page report, with three alternatives that had been thoroughly discussed. He then gave it in the hands of the general director, who had to negotiate with the three candidate firms. The project group had done its "technical job", the director now had to make a "political" decision.

The authors conclude their presentation as follows:

'The criterion for success in this action strategy is the fact that everyone can understand and follow what is being decided upon and is convinced that the most rational decision is going to be made. People therefore engage in a lot of common learning about the technical problems with which they deal. This learning is one the cognitive level. There is no evidence that learning on the socio-organisational level is going on. The project leader is guiding the process based on his expertise. It can be considered as an example of good project management.' (o.c. p. 46)

This description beautifully fits into the expert-paradigm and the concept of cognitive learning as described above. And we are not in a school but in a very modern, high-tech firm! The authors note that participants may not have learned anything on the group and organisation level. Not knowing the case, I would cast a little doubt here. They may have learned that there are two kinds of experts: those who are in the know and teach and instruct the don't-knows right to the solution of the problem, and those who know, but allow for (some) discussion and participatory decision-making. Even though this may be done for tactical reasons, it has nevertheless some influence on the organisation and its way of dealing with experts. They may also have learned, as T. Feyen indicates in her study of the introduction of new technologies and the possibilities of workers' representatives to influence the final decision, that non-specialists can exert a limited influence as to the conditions of introduction and the consequences of the new system for the people working with it (Feyen, 1992). Seeing that the final decision was left to the director, they may have learned, finally, that external experts tend to withdraw when it comes to assuming the consequences of certain decisions, and "respect the existing organisational structure".

We have reached the end of our analysis of the expert culture of education and learning. From ancient Greece down to late modern times, the power of knowledge and of expert persons and institutions divulging it has been established time and again. This was exemplified by means of Ballauff's historical analysis of the figure of the teacher, from the time of the sophists over the Middle Ages and Renaissance into our "social-technological" period. The expert paradigm of education as transmission/acquisition of solid knowledge is centred in a cognitive concept of learning and of cognitively guided instruction. Learning is like a voyage from the land of ignorance or false premises into the Land of Logos, i.e. of pure and well-established truth. In its late 20th century version, such learning is seen as a personal processing of new information, which includes at least four basic operations: comparing the new content with what is already known (the knowledge base), orienting oneself to a specific goal, building the new insight or skill into the existing network, and putting the new information in its right context. Research into learning and instruction has i.a. made us aware of the differences in learning styles and strategies, of teacher-learner interactions, of the influence of different kinds of settings upon learning.

Such a concept of education and learning is very modern indeed: it puts rationality and the individual learner's own initiative at the heart of the teaching/learning process. As we have seen, the expert paradigm is also bearer of moral expectations: expertise is the basis of an autonomous, well-informed and responsible citizenry. Thus, the pre-modern ills of sophistry, abuse of the dialogue, manipulation of the learners or oppression of the critical mind, described by Ballauff and others, would be discarded, once every person would participate in the never-ending search for evolving truth and exert his or her human rights. It was this kind of view that made the French poet Victor Hugo write: 'each school that one opens is a prison closed'. History, as we all know, has proved him wrong. This does not mean, of course, that knowledge and expertise of persons and systems should be made responsible for the ills of our world. It would be foolish to reject the advantages of modern science for society as a whole, and for education in particular. The power of knowledge and of the expert paradigm of education has been successfully reaffirmed in our time by such institutions and practices like Distance Education and the Open University, Micro teaching, Computer Assisted Teaching/Learning, Language Laboratories, Cognitively Guided Instruction, Training Within Industry, Leittext, packages for self-directed learning, etc. It should be clear that, institutionally speaking, the expert paradigm of education and learning is reaching far beyond the 4 or 8 walls of schools and universities.

At the same time, the limits of the expert model of education and learning have become increasingly clear. The research and practice examples given above are only a few instances of this "demythologisation" of the expert model. This is even true of the project on Cognitively Guided Instruction: teachers who "believe" that they are learners themselves and that you have to interact by dialogue achieve the best results with their children. Especially Rogers e.a. have shown that the successful trans-mission of ideas and procedures is highly dependent on whole sets of "antecedent" and "process variables" like personality characteristics, social values and norms, communication channels being used, interpersonal contacts, and, last, not least, the role played by the "change agent". Most important, in their model, is the clear connection-over-time of knowledge, persuasion and confirmation in the experience of the "client" adopting or rejection a new idea.

As is the case with every culture of education and learning, the expert culture has its staunch believers, who will not be altered by contrary research data or other people's experiences. In that case, humour may be the last "weapon". In a conference of directors of educational institutes held in Mexico in the winter of 1988, we heard a director-general of planning tell the long story of attempts at reform by the ministry, and its generally deceiving results. He ended his long speech with the following story:

There was a centipede who had complaints about his difficulty to move swiftly over the ground. He went to master owl, the wisest of all animals, and presented his problem: "please, offer me a solution". The owl, sitting on his high branch, turned into himself, and after a while, he spoke: "Make yourself an air cushion of 10 cm. That will allow you to walk freely and quickly. A few months later, the centipede came back, disappointed: "Master owl, I did not succeed. Could you give me some further advice?" The owl retorted, wryly: "Listen centipede, I gave you the general principle. It is up to you to work out the details".

When I told the director I had read nearly the same story in an American reader on "The planning of change" edited by Bennis e.a., back in 1964, he smiled and said: "I thought we Mexicans were the inventors of such stories"...

THE ENGINEERING CULTURE :

ACTION-ORIENTED EDUCATION CHANGES THE WORLD

From the 1960s onwards, criticism of the expert culture of education became louder and louder: modern industrial societies needed more than just the diffusion of knowledge for people to be able to solve its many problems and react to its challenges. In the terms of our centipede-story, the owl ought to come down from his high branch and become a partner-in-action.

Three aspects seemed to dominate the discussion about (adult) education: a firm belief in the autonomy and assertiveness of citizens in a "democratic society", the research-based finding that people are able and willing to learn throughout their lives, and the expectation that all major problems of man and society can be solved by means of "planned social change". Under the impulse of Unesco, at its congress in Montreal 1960, we entered the "age of éducation permanente". When all rhetoric is removed, the concept of "lifelong learning" basically comes down to the combination of two major principles:

(1) in modern democratic societies, each person has an ability and a right to fulfil his or her social, cultural, and educational needs during the whole lifetime;

(2) authorities should develop an integrated, flexible and easily accessible system of education, from Kindergarten to the "university for the third age", including provision "for a second chance" to those who missed their first chance.

Towards the end of the 1960s, an international group of experts, lead by former French minister of education Edgar Faure, set out to translate these basic but vague principles into a set of 21 more operational guidelines, illustrated each time with well-chosen examples from research and practice of the different fields of education in different continents and cultures. They published their findings in a book titled "Apprendre à Etre - Learning to be". (Faure e.a., 1973)

The global atmosphere of the 1960s was basically one of a strong belief in constant progress, as if F. Bacon's view of "effecting all things possible" would now, and finally, become a reality. Thus, sociologist Karl Mannheim, who had fled the ills of nazi-Germany, set out to revise A. Comte's famous theory of the three ages: after an initial phase of Discovery by chance or trial-and-error ("finden"), humanity passed

48

through a phase of Inventing ("erfinden") of adequate instruments or behaviour for specific needs or purposes. Most inventions, like those of the plough, the steam-engine or electricity were made that way. Gradually, and especially in the 20th century, we moved towards a phase of Planning ("Planen"), where man is no longer developing single instruments or behaviours in function of specific goals, but investigates the global connections between objects and behaviour in order to "regulate and control them". Thus, modern man will "reconstruct" his whole world (Mannheim, 1947). In other words, he becomes the engineer of his world.

Similarly, a Dutch political scientist, pleading for a "prospective" kind of policy and administration, analyzed the evolution of humankind since 1800, combining four variables: the number of books and articles being collected in libraries, the growth of income, the rising age of the population, and the increasing availability of media and means of communication. He thus presented a "curve of evolution" as follows:

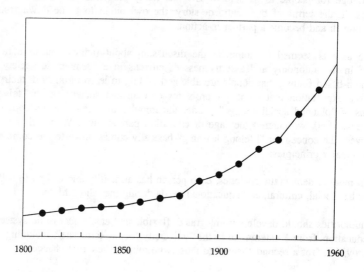

Fig. 7: The evolution of knowledge, information, income and longevity from 1800 to 1960 according to Van Duyne (Van Duyne,1966)

The decades of the 1950s and 1960s produced an avalanche of studies and research into "the planning of change". To some critics of the concept, it was merely the reflection of the post-war industrial boom, and had no solid grounds in theory. They were, in fact, wrong. One of the "grounded theories" on which the current of planned change was based was *general systems theory*, originally developed by Ludwig Von Bertalanfy for the area of biology, allowing to understand the place and evolution of living organisms, and then gradually generalised to other areas of theory and practice.

The founder of a *General Systems Theory* set as its task to unify comparable facts, laws, models and theories from the different alienated sectors of science. The Grand Dream of creating one global theory for the whole of reality - which had inspired Plato as well as Descartes and Newton - thus received a new translation.

What had started in the sphere of natural sciences soon found its way to the social sciences: in 1968, W. Buckley published a standard source book under the title: *Modern systems research for the social scientist.* (Buckley, 1968). The basic message of this still highly inspiring book was that general systems theory had produced a *Systems Approach*, i.e. a proper frame of reference and a vision on physical as well as social reality: the phenomena of reality cannot be seen as isolated objects, but can only be fully understood if they are looked upon as systems or parts of systems. One of the most concise definitions of system given in the book sounded as follows: 'a system is a collection of objects together with the relationships between these objects and between their characteristics' (Buckley, o.c. p. 81). This definition already contains two of the basic properties of a system: *totality* or wholeness and *interrelation* or connectedness of all elements with one another. From the initial literature, one can deduce four other characteristics: *goal orientation* or the dynamic striving for realising specific effects, *planned order* or structuration according to a definite arrangement, *delimitation* or the existence of a border between the system and its environment, and *hierarchical structure* of two or more subsystems within an encompassing supra-system.

What some people called "systemology" seemed to offer an interesting but fairly abstract model for understanding complex realities. The pragmatic value of the systems approach became clear when a group of authors, under the direction of W. G. Bennis, set out to synthesize the whole field of planned social change in 1964, and introduced a simplified system approach for all attempts to bring about changes in individuals, groups, organisations and whole societies. An effort at planned change was described as the organisation of a temporary *inter-system*, whereby an *agent-system*, possessing expertise, tried to realise desired changes in a *client-system*, which experienced the need for such a change.

Education was simply one of the many areas, where this model could be applied. In fact, this meant the introduction of the engineering paradigm in the field of education: educators became *change agents*, possessing both content and process knowledge, entering in interaction with (groups of) *clients*, who expressed or were made aware of their learning needs, and would start working strategically at effecting the desired change with the help of the agent- or service-system. Great attention was paid also to the *environment* in which the change process took place, and especially to the problems of resistance to change and of transfer of learning effects to the "back home" situation.

During the planning phase of the action-research project already mentioned in the previous chapter, we found a gratifying model in this systems approach. We roughly considered the KAV-organisation, and especially the national work group leading the project, as a "service system" which would develop programmes and actions for and with the "client system" of local sections and their membership. The supra-system was simply the whole organisation with its national board, national secretariat, its 17 districts and its 1050 local sections. We even defined local leaders as "our clients" becoming, in turn, "change agents" for their own local "clients". At that time, it provided us with a mental model for understanding, planning and evaluating the whole project. Only twelve years later, while constructing a process theory for adult education, did we look more closely into the basic characteristics and implications of systems theory, and developed a proper systems theory for adult education as "an open growth system". (Leirman & Vandemeulebroecke, 1984). As early as 1968, the systems approach was being translated to (adult) education theory in such countries like the Netherlands and Germany. The same was true for the whole area of school education and the comparative study of "national systems", where different definitions of system were in use. (Mesdom & Wielemans, 1979). Especially Dutch authors, like M. Van Beugen, did their best to introduce what they called *social technology*: education was seen as "instrumental agogical action", following a 6-step strategy, from "diagnosing or stimulating a need for change" down to "evaluation". (Van Beugen, 1972). He made use of the earlier work on 'the dynamics of planned change' by Lippitt e.a. (Lippitt, 1958), who were themselves students of the "first engineer of planned change", Kurt Lewin.

Table 3: Strategic Educational Action according to Lewin and Lippitt cs.

K. LEWIN (*Frontiers of group dynamics, 1947*)	R. LIPPITT e.a. (*Dynamics of planned change, 1958*)
A. UNFREEZING OF FIXED BEHAVIOUR	1. AWARENESS OF A NEED TO CHANGE 2. ESTABLISHING A CHANGE RELATIONSHIP
B. MOVING TO NEW GOAL	3. CLARIFICATION AND DIAGNOSIS OF THE PROBLEM 4. EXPLORING ALTERNATIVE ROADS, DETERMINING GOALS AND DEVELOPING A WORK PLAN 5. EXECUTION OF PLAN FOR CHANGE
C. (Re)FREEZING OR CONSOLIDATING NEW BEHAVIOUR	6. GENERALISATION AND STABILISATION - EVALUATION 7. TERMINATION OF RELATIONSHIP

Lewin, having fled nazi-Germany, discovered the problems of social minorities in the USA, and became highly interested in the question of changing the attitudes of people in a desired, more "democratic" direction. In his study on group processes of 1947, he stated that, for change to be effective, groups had to go through three phases: one of "unfreezing" existing rigid ideas and beliefs, of "moving" towards a new behaviour, and of "refreezing" or consolidating the newly acquired behaviour. The engineering language being used was no coincidence, since Lewin was, next to being a social psychologist, also an engineer. On the basis of their study of 400 "change projects" in industry and professional organisations, Lippitt e.a. broadened Lewin's client-perspective, by introducing the *relationship change agent-client* into the process model, and by breaking it down into 7 steps, as is indicated in the table on the next page.

In the 1960s and the 1970s, countless variants were constructed to Lewin's and Lippitt's process schemes. Authors changed the order of phases, added new phases to them, but basically the outlook remained the same: education was strategic action for change.

Let us now illustrate this engineering culture of education with a first research example. We are talking here again about the P.O.M-project, described in the previous chapter. We now present it in its global, and action-oriented framework. The national committee of the KAV-organisation had published a manifesto about the emancipation of women, pleading i.a. for a greater participation of women in all areas of public life, and for a better education of girls, away from the "traditional patterns of home economics". They were more or less shocked to hear that a content analysis of 20 group discussions among the men's branch of the christian workers' association revealed a clearly discriminatory attitude towards the education of girls: "boys should study longer in order to get good jobs, girls do not need that, since their task is to educate children and to look after the household". (Lagrou & Laforce, 1971)

The KAV-leadership asked for a meeting with representatives of two university sections: Applied Social Psychology and Adult Education. They wanted us to do research "in order to promote workers' women and girls' emancipation". We listened, and then proposed to set up a project in two phases: first, the social psychologists would gauge the attitude of the members of the association regarding educational opportunities for girls, and in a next phase, the adult education unit would work with the membership, starting from the research data.

In Table 4 on the next page, we present the overall plan for the project, specifying phases, contents/programmes, target groups and the global time schedule. That plan was described and extensively justified in a long article which we published at the beginning of the actual project. (Leirman, 1971)

In phase one, we drew a random sample of 25 local sections, who had a total membership of 2510 members. A 6-point attitude scale of 36 items was developed around 6 major topics. The first item sounded: "Girls who study for a long time often become bad housewives"... Members were invited to express their opinion by choosing between " 1 = very right"... to " 6 = totally wrong". We received a response of 56% of the members of the sample. At the same time, the questionnaire was distributed to the remaining 1050 sections, and 47% of these sent a total of 48.000 questionnaires back to the national secretariat.

The data of the random sample were factor-analyzed, and we found six new factors, like "A girl better be sure of a good result at school, or else she can stay home with her mother" and "further education alienates girls from their working parents". At the

Table 4: Design of the Project "Educational Opportunities for Working Class Girls"

PHASES -->	SOCIAL-PSY-CHOLOGICAL	SOCIAL - PEDAGOGICAL		
		PLANNING AND PROGRAMMING		CONSCIEN-TISATION AND ACTION
CONTENTS ->	ATTITUDE RESEARCH IN SAMPLE OF 2500 MEMBERS CONTENT ANALYSIS OF 20 GROUP DISCUSSIONS	A 2 SESSIONS OF INFORMATION AND TRAINING WITH LEADERS, ANIMATORS AND STUDENTS	C 2 PROGRAM-MING SESSIONS IN LOCAL UNIT	EXECUTION
		B INFORMATION FOR MEMBERS	D PRESENTA-TION OF PROGRAM OFFER TO MEMBERS	REGIONAL & NATIONAL ACTION
TIME	OCT.'68 - JAN.'71	JANUARY '71 -	SEPT. '71	OCT.'71 - OCT. '73
PARTICI-PANTS	SAMPLE OF 26 LOCAL SECTIONS	15 LOCAL SECTIONS		KAV AS WHOLE MOVEMENT

same time, we found strong disagreement among members about items like the one cited above. It was clear that the membership did not think as "progressively" as the national committee.

Disposing of these data, we then convened and planned the second, so-called socio-pedagogical phase. After long and sometimes difficult discussions, we first established the general objectives of the "action" phase:

1. To give people from the working class a chance to exchange and justify their opinions about further education for girls, making use, i.a. of the research data of the first phase

2. To let them explore the situation and the development of secondary education for girls at the regional and the national level

3. To help them to recognise their own wants and needs and the hindrances in relation to a responsible participation in education

4. To set up (a) programmes and (b) develop actions together with these people in order to solve their problems (change of mentality and of structures)

5. Thus to contribute to the development of girls and women from the working class as full-fledged partners in society .

Each of these general objectives was then operationalised into between 5 and 8 specific so-called "work-goals".

In the table, one can see that the action phase was in itself subdivided into two steps, according to the objectives: preparatory information, training, programme planning and programme presentation by local leaders (obj. 1-4a), followed by execution of programmes and actions (4b - 5). For research purposes, we split the random sample into two groups: 15 units where we would systematically prepare programmes and train "animators" and "local leaders" to carry them out (the so-called a-sections), and 11 units which would follow the "normal" national programme, without special preparation (the so-called b-sections). Because of the newness of it all, we first did a test of the new approach in a group of 16 other local sections, which proved its feasibility, but lead to a number of changes in the overall project plan.

The plan was carried out in most of the local sections as foreseen, whereas the association as a whole also chose to work on the issue of furthering educational opportunities for working class girls and parent participation. For that purpose, we worked out a "workbook" for local sections, and diffused the research data of the first phase by means of a slide projection programme and sets of wall-papers, show-ing the six factors and the opinion of the membership in popular form. The figure on the next page shows the content of the first factor about the girl "better staying in the household, unless she obtains good results", and the general distribution of "pros" and "cons" in the membership. In order to promote discussion of these factors and their underlying attitudes, we constructed a "discussion game", whereby members were divided into groups of four, receiving each a set of 6 cards, from 1= "totally disagree" to 6 = "totally agree". They were asked to listen carefully to the item, privately make a choice of an opinion card, showing this to the group and discussing their opinion and that of the others for 8 to 10 minutes. After the discussion, they were asked to score the item again. We tape-recorded 10 % of all discussions, and analyzed their content.

The project was about more than personal opinions, however, as the goal statements above indicate. Therefore, we proposed several action possibilities and discussed them with our 15 sections. They decided to work towards greater participation of workers' women in local school boards c.q. parents' associations. But once local leaders had come to an agreement about the "action theme", they started expressing their apprehension: how could they face school directors or teachers, what possibilities did they have for entering parent's committees, etc? We therefore decided to offer them a "special preparation" in the form of a simulation game which we called "parents' participation in the school of Zegem" (Dutch for "tell-him"). We invited all local presidents or local project leaders together with their professional "animators" - a total group of 32 persons - and divided them in 5 "role-groups": local school board, teachers, KAV-committee, working class parents and "other parents". In four rounds of one hour each, we explored the problem of setting up a local parents' committee through repeated negotiations between the different parties involved. During the evaluation of the day-long game, which lead to the decision to start a parents' organisation, we asked participants about their experiences. Apart from the fact that they had enjoyed this type of "action game", most of them stated that they now had a far better understanding of the complexity of the problem and saw the different implications of certain decisions, but only one third of them said that they were "less afraid to really take action in their local community". Finally, five of the fifteen experimental sections deployed some kind of action around the chosen topic.

At the end of the project, we repeated the opinion research both in the KAV-sample and in a control group of 250 non-members, and found out that the attitude of KAV-members had changed in the direction the organisation had hoped for, and that their attitude was at the same time significantly more positive than that of the control group.

Looking upon this project from the model of adult education described above, it is clear that it shows most of the characteristics of the so-called *socio-technological* or *engineering* concept: both the national committee and we as researchers acted as "change agents" trying to influence the knowledge and, above all, the attitude of the "clients" in a more "progressive direction", an effort which proved to be successful, both in the A - and in the B-sections. In fact, there was a certain tension here between the "official" and the "real" goals. The official attitudinal goal stated that we wanted to offer people from the working class an opportunity to exchange and justify

Figure 8: Representation of the content and the KAV-members' opinion on factor 1 (project 'Educational Opportunities for Working Class Girls', 1971)

56

their attitude about education for girls, using the results of the opinion research, but the leadership of the organisation, and most of the researchers hoped that there would indeed occur a change "in the direction of greater emancipation".

However, the so-called "action phase" contained more than just the preparation and execution of an "action strategy". Several local groups discovered that they themselves were capable of developing their own programmes, instead of just "picking out the items presented by the national secretariat". At the same time, some of the professional "animators" developed a new, more horizontal style of communicating with local chapters, instead of, as one told us, "trying to sell to them the offerings of the national association". In other words: the dependency of some local sections upon their professional "animators" and the "top" of the organisation was reduced, and that was something that we from the university had hoped for, but had never dared to formulate in terms of explicit goals. What we had done, was propose the following statement in the basic document: 'adult education operates in a tension field of two extremes one should avoid: the extreme of dogmatic knowledge diffusion and forced change of attitudes and structures on the one hand, and the other extreme of laissez-faire offerings and of waiting for spontaneous development and action to occur. In the actual situation, we are most often closer to the first than to the second extreme...The ideology has changed, however: from a position of conscientisation, action and conquest from the top downward, one nowadays stresses such principles as democratisation, participation and co-determination. The P.O.M.-project is operating within the latter principles' (o.c. p. 3). A final evaluation of the project in 1977 proved that this was generally true, but at the same time, we discovered that the organisation as such had not generally applied these principles, e.g. in the way local programmes were developed. Symbolically speaking, one might say that "the educators-engineers had left the scene, and had not found local imitators".

The approach described thus far bears a clear semblance to what Bouwen and Fry call "the sales model" of organisational innovation and learning. Here, the leader-innovator acts as "sales person" trying to persuade his clientele of the importance of the newly proposed idea or procedure, keeps showing and demonstrating its uses and advantages, tries to develop a good interaction climate, carefully plans every step, and sees to it that a high rate of adoption among the clients is attained. (Bouwen, 1992, p. 44 f.)

Let us look at the case example given by them. BANK is a medium-sized savings bank, which has decided to introduce a new scoring system for its clients. The initiative comes from the EDP-manager - who has developed the new computing programme for scoring clients. He installs a work group composed of representatives of central services and a number of local branch offices. Collaboration of the latter is crucial: they have to provide the data to work on and are the major users in contact with clients. However, the information service department wants to control the composition of the scoring system, so that it cannot be manipulated by local agents.

The project leader is considered to be the "product champion" of the new system, which he developed with his technical staff. At the same time, he works hard towards what he calls a consensus orientation in the project group. He is an active discussion leader, emphasizing principles and common interests: the new system has to be both "commercial" for the clients and "safe" for the bank. He acknowledges the contributions of all members, creates a positive atmosphere during the meetings, and tries to keep the balance between critical participation on the one hand and safeguarding what he considers to be the essential characteristics of the new scoring system on the other. One of the group members describes his behaviour as follows: "He is competent, very fluent and intelligent. It gives him an aura of excellence. But it is very difficult to stop him."

When group members say that the *scoring system is very new*, he understates this by telling them "you have been doing this, in fact, for years, we are only formalising it". He also tries to avoid to progress too quickly. A project group member from a local agency speaks positively about the project group as a case of "oiling the machinery" of the central services in their relation to external agencies. A first result of the project group is that its function is *institutionalised* as a "department" close to the president, with the project leader as direct advisor. A second outcome is an organisation-wide acceptance of the scoring system, and further development of other tools to "support" or "guide" the work in local agencies.

This story shows indeed a "salesman" at work: he works towards acceptance by the users, asks for their continuous commitment and persuades them to take action. Looking back at the case, the authors make the following final comment: 'The whole project's group work can be considered as an action to help the organisation to digest slowly the introduction of central information and control devices... All objections and reactions are taken into consideration, but the original principles are never changed. The eventual promotion of the project leader makes the acceptance easier, but illustrates at the same time that the active mechanism in the action strategy is more *benevolent acceptance* than critical contribution and personal learning.' (o.c., p. 45)

The latter remark contains in fact an implicit reference to the *nature and the effectiveness of the power* used by the project leader. The power base in use is of a double nature: on the one hand, the project leader takes advantage of his technical expertise, and on the other hand he uses his legitimate position in the hierarchy as one who is close to the top management and represents the interests of the whole organisation. *Legitimate* power is combined here with *expert* power, in that order. This power-combination is gradually different from what we could observe in the expert-model, where expert knowledge appeared to be of prime importance, eventually in combination with the legitimate position of the educators in their institutions.

In describing the process as he experiences it, one participant uses a highly illuminating image: "oiling the machinery". This may well be the most adequate metaphor to describe what the engineering model is basically about, namely to heighten the effec-

58

tiveness of the organisation and the people working in it: a better scoring system for the bank, a new way of programming in the cultural movement, a new division of tasks, a greater ability at taking appropriate action, etc. Therefore, the type of learning occurring under such a model is sometimes referred to as *instrumental learning*.

In a broader perspective, C. Argyris has termed the behaviour of an organisation operating under the pre-cited conditions as *model I- behaviour*. (Argyris & Schön, 1987) This is characterised by the following features:

- goals are determined unilaterally (usually by the "top")
- control over execution of tasks is equally unilateral
- one makes statements which cannot be tested and/or contradicted
- one avoids to rouse negative feelings
- one tries to "save one's face" and not make a negative impression

The values underlying such a behaviour are: win-don't-lose, rational goal orientation, central control. Consequences of model-I action are basically negative: mistakes remain hidden, information is withheld or thwarted, defensiveness...

Groups of people and organisations operating according to such a model - and apparently this is the case for the majority of them - only reach short-term effects, and can only solve routine problems.

Argyris and Schön oppose a *model-II*, which contradicts in almost every respect the processes and characteristics described above. We will discuss this "ideal" model later on. Presenting these models once before an audience, Argyris stated that many people advocate the latter model, but act according to the first one: their "espoused theory" is different from their "theory in use". This difference has long been known as the difference between the teachings of a preacher and his actual deeds...

Does all this boil down to a condemnation of the engineering model of education? We think a caveat is well in place. First of all, researchers into learning and learning processes keep saying that there are different types of learners and different styles of learning. Thus, D.A. Kolb, in exploring the dynamics of experiential learning, distinguishes four types of learning which, together, constitute a full-fledged learning cycle, yet with clear differences in weight and sequence:

- concrete *experiencing* is often the first step: people are often confronted with aspects of reality first of all in the form of emotionally coloured experiences;
- this is often followed by *reflexive observation*, i.e. thinking about the meaning(s) of one's experiences;
- from there, one may move into *abstract conceptualisation*, i.e. formulating principles, rules and even theories deduced from observations;
- finally, there may take place *active experimentation*, in the form of applying the precited rules and principles. (Kolb, 1984)

Kolb keeps insisting, however, that this sequence is not always being followed, and that specific steps may be highly reduced. Thus, experimentation is not always the application of rules and principles learned before! Equally, human persons do evolve during their learning history, and some people appear to be stronger in one type of learning than in another one. In analogy to the four types of learning, Kolb distinguishes four types of learners:

(1) *dreamers* or people who are keen on making new experiences in open and unstructured situations where they can act creatively;
(2) *thinkers* or persons interested in solving problems and understanding their backgrounds so that they can develop new ideas;
(3) *deciders* who prefer a well-structured learning situation with an accent on solid information, which they can then apply in an exercise;
(4) *doers* or persons interested in practical applicability of information provided.

Even though one may doubt the well-foundedness of such a typology, it helps us to understand that the engineering model of education may find a positive response from two types of learners: the "deciders" and, above all, the "doers". Furthermore, research into training and learning in Dutch industry reveals that differences in learning style are linked to differences in professions: "dreamers" are encountered above all in personnel sections and with trainers, "thinkers" seem to find a home above all in research and accountancy units, "deciders" are found in production units - and among them especially the engineers - and "doers" seem to be active in outreaching professions like marketing and sales. (Lindeboom & Peeters, 1986).

Concurrently, the engineering model has a clear methodological preference for what was first called "action-research", and, later on, "action-oriented" research. The central focus here is not on testing a theoretically founded hypothesis and clarifying the relationships between variables, but on helping to solve existing problems and developing theories-of-action. This means, in terms introduced by De Munter, that a "plan-model" of a given situation, which allows us to map and understand it, is linked to a "helping-model", which specifies those aspects which educator(s) can try to change. (De Munter, 1976, p. 47 f.). De Munter therefore makes a distinction between "situation variables" like gender or age, which one cannot influence, and "decision variables", like knowledge of X or attitude versus Y, which can be influenced by the educational process. Action-oriented research is a special form of developing a "helping-model", since the researcher(s) help to select the decision variables, as well as the strategies and methods of influencing them. In system theory terms, they become partner-change agents, who cooperate with practitioners in setting up a service-system for the clients or participants. At the same time, however, they "keep their distance", since they are clearly interested in analyzing and evaluating the whole process, and in deriving rules or principles for other types of change processes. With a reference to Kolb's typology, they take up the "dreamer-thinker" as well as the "decider-doer" roles, albeit with different weight during the evolution of the process. This, of course, is not the easiest of positions. We will come back to this double-bind in the next chapter.

Action-orientation at a local level is, as we have seen, a key characteristic of the engineering model. It came, also, as a reaction to the predominance of a rational and cognitivistic approach in the expert model. An area where this transition became clearly visible is that of school reform and school innovation. Originally, school reform was seen from a mere "adoption-perspective", where the innovation is viewed as a rational construct, which has to be diffused to local schools and teachers as passive receivers and executors of pre-planned packages. Berman termed this *the technological-experimental* paradigm. (Berman, 1981 in Staessens, 1990). Empirical research into such diffusion efforts revealed a great gap between the original plans and the variances in (non)-application at the local level. As a reaction, far greater stress was put on the interaction between the innovation plan and the local school setting. This perspective was called *mutual adaptation* : 'an organisational process in which an innovative plan is developed and modified in light of the realities of the institutional setting, and in which the organisation changes to meet the requirements of the innovation project' (Staessens, o...c. p. 3, p. 392 f.). Within this perspective, the innovators work together with the local school teams to realise the blueprint-in-an-adapted form.

That seemed to be the initial basic philosophy of a huge innovation project in the domain of grammar schools in Flanders, called   " Renewed Grammar School Education (V.L.O)", started in 1980. In it, great attention was paid to aspects like promotion of team work and constant reflection on school praxis and school policy (Vandenberghe & Depoortere, 1986). A first global evaluation showed that there were four different types of reaction to the innovation project, a finding which corroborated the conclusion that local schools should each develop their own type of innovation policy. One of the questions raised at this point was: how can we understand and explain such local differences? A global proposition to answer this question was that a difference in the degree of implementation of school innovation would be directly related to differences in *local professional culture*. This concept became very popular in the beginning of the 1980s, when the success of Japanese industry was explained by referring to their special "corporate culture" of "working as one family by consensual decision-making", in contrast to the hierarchical structure and the highly fragmented division of tasks in western industry.

In her research project, K. Staessens set out to study the "degree of implementation of the V.L.O. innovation" in 116 schools, and then did an in-depth study in 9 schools with clearly different profiles in terms of implementation. It was here that special attention was paid to the local professional culture, defined as 'the basic assumptions which are being shared by the members of an organisation, which operate unconsciously, and which contain a self-evident definition of the vision of the organisation upon itself and its environment ' (Staessens, o.c. p. 393). For the expression of this culture, three specific domains were selected: the profile of the director of the school, the basic goal-orientation or 'mission' of the school, and the professional relations within the teachers' teams.

The comparative analysis of interviews and observations lead to the discovery of three different school types, for which three metaphors were used, linked to the basic goal orientation:

- the *family-school* with a culture of cosiness and togetherness, expressed in the assumption: 'we are a nice group with good intentions. We can be confident that things will run smoothly and spontaneously here';
- the *school as professional institution* with a culture stressing professional expertise: 'we have an important task to fulfil';
- the *living-apart-together school* (Lat), characterised by a culture of mediocrity: 'Let's be just a school like any other'.

Each of these school types appeared to have a specific type of director and school team as well: the "family-school" had a "grandfather"-kind of director acting as friend and partner, and a team working like a "village music band", trying to keep alive and to survive; the "professional school" had the "architect-type" of director working as a professional leader and builder of a well-functioning school, and a team acting like a "professional soccer club" with constant care for effectiveness of the school as a whole; the LAT-school had an "invisible" type of director and a "loose-sand-team " guided by the principle 'Only count on yourself'.

Not surprisingly perhaps, it was the "professional school" that appeared to offer the highest degree of implementation of the V.L.O. goals, followed by the "family school" with a medium, and the LAT-school with a weak degree of implementation.

The research project on professional innovation cultures was concluded with a case study of one such "professional school", symbolically called here "the Cornflower". One of the things that struck this reader's attention most strongly was the development of a so-called *school-workplan* on 'continuity in reading' throughout the grammar school. This was divided into a "vertical" and a "horizontal" work scheme. By "vertical" they meant the phasing-over-time, by "horizontal" the division of tasks among colleagues.

The elaborate vertical scheme provided a step-by-step action spread out over the 10 months of a normal school year, as follows:

OBSERVATION 1

> *1. Information and discussion session on observation of the reading process*
> *2. Observation period*
> *3. Evaluation of first observation*

DISCUSSION OF READING MATERIALS

> *Analysis of actual and of desired situation (materials on reading method and remediation)*

OBSERVATION 2

     1. Period of specific guidance combined with observation
     2. Evaluation

PROCEDURE FOR CHILDREN NEEDING SPECIAL GUIDANCE

     1. Information and discussion session
     2. Meeting of central team
     3. Elaboration of procedure for 'special guidance'
     4. Fill in guidance diary
     5. Evaluation

DISCUSSION ABOUT TRANSFER TO NEXT GRADE

     1. Fill in observation scheme for children of 3rd year kindergarten
     2. Testing children 3rd year kindergarten
     3. Discussion about transfer in multi-disciplinary team
     4. Discussion of transfer between successive grades/classes

FINAL EVALUATION

     Evaluation of planned action

It took the school two years to implement this whole workplan, which shows the characteristics of the "unfreezing, moving - refreezing" model explained above. Its most important result was the introduction of "different reading-level groups", according to the reading ability of the children in each class, and hence the possibility to give each child an opportunity to learn according to its capacities. At the same time, parents received more detailed information about the actual and the possible level of their child. The director, who had chosen this as a priority for his school, closely supervised the whole process, and even asked a teacher, who was reluctant to implement the new plan, to go and observe the application of this scheme in a colleague's class. He thus realised complete adoption 'because there can be no laggards. Everybody must cooperate'. At the end of the case study period, a teacher states 'we have now come out of our separate boxes, and are talking more with one another', and the director concluded that 'a new pattern of reflection' had been introduced, meaning that 'we now evaluate ourselves, every teacher in his/her class, and every class in comparison to the whole group, without this being a threat'. (Staessens, o..c., p. 380 f.)

From what precedes, we can conclude that the so-called professional school bears many of the characteristics of the engineering model: the director acts as a strong leader using his legitimate as well as his expert power, the relationship between him and the teachers is coloured by the common task, there is a continuous planning in regular, functionally oriented team meetings, a strong accent is put on reflexive action, there is a "refreezing" of results in the form of concrete procedures and materials implemented throughout the school. From the viewpoint of the innovation project, the "Cornflower" looks like a "model school", and some teachers state "we are working here like one big family". Yet, professional culture has its price as well: at lunch time, the teachers split into two groups. One group takes its lunch packet in the premises of the kindergarten, and consists of teachers who do have some problems with the "functional, somewhat impersonal" behaviour of the director. The other group takes its (warm) meal together with the director in the main building: these teachers appear to fully support the director. A systems approach makes one wonder, furthermore, about the relationship between the school and its environment in the present and in the past. The case study pays clear attention to this aspect: the "Cornflower" was started in 1963 in a rather inimical environment, and the first ten years were a period of "fighting and pioneering". Luckily, the fact that a new neighbourhood was constructed near the school where young families came to live, its being situated in a beautiful landscape, and the fact that the original "barracks" were replaced by a modern new building all played a role in its full expansion after ten years. Thus, the professional culture inside was much helped by the social and material culture outside.

The case study also brings into focus a party or subsystem which had hitherto been left out of the picture: the pupils. At the time of the study, i. e.. after 25 years of school life, the pupils seem to play an active role in the school, since they have been working for a whole year on a "total show about the school's history and functioning", which was received with great enthusiasm by parents, the "friends' circle" and former students. Next to this group culture, there is also growing attention for differentiation - as we saw in the continuity of reading project - and for individual guidance. Yet, classes of pupils as such seldom come into focus - and we all know that their "culture" may be very different from one group to another and from one year to another year. The same can be said of parents, who seem to be the silent witnesses of the whole process. The V.L.O.- philosophy takes parent participation as one of its priorities, however. But of course, a researcher cannot study all (sub)systems at once, and school systems have their hierarchical structure, where director and teachers' team are key masters in the game.

The use of well-phrased metaphors is a strong feature of the study, but the author is also aware of its danger: it conjures up rich connotations, but at the same time, it may work as a stereotypic label, especially in negatively coloured expressions like "living apart together school", "grand-pa director", "figurative director" and "loose-sand-team". An English school supervisor, working with so-called "community-schools" in Oxfordshire, whom we visited in 1976 because we had received information about two "pioneer schools" in his district, received us with an ironic remark: "You come to visit schools with a good reputation. You know, reputations are always exaggerated, either for the good or for the bad".

In the P.O.M.-project described above, we had long discussions about how we would present, both visually and verbally, the attitudinal factors to the membership, knowing that opinions were highly divided, and that we might unnecessarily hurt people's feelings. Especially the KAV-leadership was sensitive to that problem. Thus, we did not say "girls who study for a long time betray their parents", but spoke of "become strangers", and showed a girl who left her parents' house smilingly. In one case, however, we used the expression "bossing housewife", because that expression was used in two of the attitude scale-items. During the many discussions in local groups, we never received any serious remarks about the use of images and popular expressions. Maybe, our long experienced partners knew well enough the "culture of their local sections" to tune our messages to them accordingly.

The precited study reveals the importance of professional, or rather organisational, cultures for the success or failure of educational innovation projects in schools. We consider this as an important contribution to our own analysis. The model of education and learning under scrutiny here - for which we also use a metaphor - appears to be linked to an organisational culture which was captured in terms like "professional institution", "functional task orientation", "director-architect" and "teachers-football team".

Upon retrospect, we can apply some of these metaphors to the KAV-organisation with which we worked for 5 years. In this case, we are unable to reach one global conclusion. The top of the organisation - and especially the professional supervisors - could be equally characterised as a "professional institution" with an outspoken task-orientation and a will to increase the effectiveness of the organisation, internally as well as externally. In the so-called "basis" - the local sections - the situation we encountered was far more diversified. The majority of sections could be categorised as "family groups", who, as we once stated, "celebrated their existence and their togetherness", and looked upon the project with an eclectic eye, selecting those items which were convergent with their "family culture", e.g. the presentation of the slides with the results and some informative items. A second group came close to the "professional culture" and immediately perceived the P.O.M.-project as a local action project on parent participation. They realised the Adoption phase in the innovation-decision process to a fair degree. A third group did not engage themselves in any significant way and did not even enter the innovation process, but we are not sure whether we could label them as "LAT"-sections: sometimes there was a lack of dynamism in the local direction committee, so that the membership was never solicited, sometimes they had other interests or priorities, and sometimes, indeed, the committee lacked leadership and coherence or went through an internal conflict.

The different examples given above have gradually provided us with an insight in the contours of what we have called the engineering culture of education and learning. The basic vision behind this culture is that of *homo faber*, man as architect or artisan of his own world, and of a *professionalised society*, with a culture stressing skilful planned action and effectiveness. The 'mission' of education is to guide learners to such a level of qualification that they become skilful 'professional' actors, and learn to function together as effective teams or organisations. The preferred strategy can be called social-technological, since it accentuates dynamic cooperative planning and technically perfect execution under strong leadership. The heavy accent on planning brings the engineering model fairly close to the expert model, yet the difference between the two is clarified when we look at the underlying concept of learning. Here, learning is not so much a process of cognitive problem-solving, but rather of transformation of action structures. Simply stated, the focus is on "learning by doing" as John Dewey explained with great emphasis. Accordingly, the position of the educator is not in the first place that of the didactician and the informant, but of the architect and the process manager in an attempt at planned change.

Kolb's distinction of four types of learners described above, makes us aware of the fact that especially the "decider" and the "doer"-type may profit most from the engineering model of education.

Here, we come upon the limits of this model. In organisational cultures of the "family"- or the isolated "LAT"-type, the engineering model will have far less impact than in the so-called "professional" cultures. Furthermore, the "dreamers" and the "thinkers" may not find in it sufficient stimuli to "muse and ponder", and may feel too strong a pressure to engage in what they see as premature action.

The examples given above may create the impression that the engineering model is a post-World War II construction. This would be an unjustified conclusion. Historically speaking, the engineering model has a long tradition. One example is the medieval institution of the training of apprentices under the supervision of a "master" within the framework of a professional guild. This was one of the earliest instances of what is called nowadays "learning in the workplace". (Marsick, 1987) The bakery, butchery, brewery, the carpenter's workshop were not schools, there were no handbooks, but apprentices did learn a trade by following the instructions and the example of the master, or of those who had already passed their first test as a "companion". There certainly were moments of systematic instruction or explanation about general principles, the nature of materials or technical procedures, but these were rather rare, and not planned in curricular order. (Carton, 1984)

Until the 18th century, handicrafts, trades and professions in general had a fairly restricted and unaltered profile. The explosion of knowledge in the "new" sciences, the first industrial revolution and the division of labour created a movement of what Van Onna has called "divergence" between labour and education: workplaces could no longer execute the educative tasks, especially in the domains of general knowledge and skills, which were relegated to vocational/technical schools. (Van Onna, 1985 & 1992). After World War II, the need for (re)training of the workforce in industry and the expansion and changes in trades and commerce lead to the development of a panoply of so-called "off-the-job"-training programmes. According to Van Onna, they have four basic characteristics:

(1) comprehensiveness of the training, in relation to the qualification profile of the intended profession or function;

(2) possibility to plan (parts of) the training programme on beforehand;

(3) theoretical foundation with a minimum of regular theoretical instruction;

(4) individual guidance of the learner, with regard to the learning trajectory and the degree of specialisation.

The expansion of both vocational-technical school education and off-the-job training programmes could not prevent criticisms and doubts on behalf of industry and the professions: lack of relevancy to practice, outdatedness of information, lack of insight in the work organisation and the work culture, lack of professional attitudes, insufficient opportunities for exercises were some of the most frequently heard remarks and complaints.

Therefore, many professional organisations developed programmes and systems of "on-the-job" or directly work-related training. The expectation was that the precited problems could be avoided or reduced to a bearable minimum. In the 60s and the 70s, one saw two different types of programmes in operation. Van Onna compares the two types in the table on the next page.
The author himself, and many commentators after him, state that we cannot speak here of a radical difference between two contradictory systems, but rather of a continuum from "Arbeitsplatznähe" or "closeness to the workplace" to "Arbeitsplatz-ferne" or "remoteness from the workplace". Moreover, it is not so much the "learning place" which is important, but rather the fundamental orientation. In this sense, the terms "on-the-job" and "off-the-job" are misleading. Anyhow, the table verbalises six dimensions or semantic scales: improvisation-planning, occasionality-systematisation, production-orientation versus educational orientation, specialisation-generalisation, actuality-future perspective and concretisation-theoretisation. De Vries even added a seventh dimension: integration-fragmentation (De Vries, 1988).

"Off-the-job" training reveals a very "schoolish" face, and comes very close to what we called the expert model of systematic diffusion of knowledge and skills. The "on-the-job" training shows far more "work" characteristics than educational traits. Therefore, it cannot be well compared with our engineering model of education, with the exception perhaps of its orientation to concrete local action and integration in the work environment. The fact that "on-the-job" training has such a low educational profile is of course due to its subservience to the work and production logic: there is no time to lose, work must go on! In some situations, it would even be dangerous to interrupt the production process for systematic instruction. Some critical commentators therefore wonder how one can speak here of *training*, if it all comes down to spontaneity and incidental learning. De Vries therefore speaks of *three types* of learning processes: non-organised learning processes or informal learning, organised

Table 6: Characteristics of on-the-job and off-the-job training (adapted from: Van Onna, 1985)

ON-THE-JOB	OFF-THE-JOB
SPONTANEOUS LEARNING (improvisation)	INTENTIONAL LEARNING (planning)
INCIDENTAL LEARNING IN WORK PROCESS (occasionality)	SYSTEMATIC DIDACTICAL ORGANISATION (systematisation)
PRODUCTION ORIENTED (economisation)	LEARNER ORIENTED (pedagogisation)
SPECIALISATION ACCORDING TO DIVISION OF LABOUR (specialisation)	GENERALISATION: BROAD KNOWLEDGE AND SKILLS (generalisation)
SITUATION-BOUND (actualization)	COURSE-BOUND (future perspective)
DIRECT APPLICATION (concretisation)	GENERAL EDUCATION (theoretisation)

learning processes within the work situation and organised learning processes outside of the work environment. (De Vries, o.c., p. 91). This well-founded differentiation implies that we should reorder the table above into a three-category scheme: *On-the job learning, on-the-job training* and *off-the-job training.*

This reordering does not diminish, however, the differences, and even the tension between the "work logic" and the "school logic". Since the end of the 1960s, special efforts have been made at linking the different orientations together, e.g. in the "dual system" of work experience and vocational education for youngsters in Germany, the system of "alternance" between work and school in France, and the "apprenticeship system" and "partial instruction" in Belgium (Jallade, 1988, De Waele e.a., 1988). These and other efforts are seen by Van Onna as expressions of a 'movement of convergence' between work and learning/education. In actual practice, they come down to a division of 3-4 days at work, mostly under the direction of a supervisor or a professional, and 1-2 days at school or in an educational centre, with a mixed programme of general education and some vocational training. In a more theoretical perspective, we might say that what is looked for is a combination of the engineering and the expert model.

According to De Vries, who carefully analyzed the different systems of vocational education for youngsters in the Netherlands, and the theoretical models behind them, this dream of integration cannot be realised. He formulates the following proposition:

'The widely diffused idea that theoretical learning at school and practical learning in professional practice can be meaningfully integrated within one curriculum is wrong and should be regarded as one of the myths guiding school innovation of the last decades.... This proposition is also applicable to the apprenticeship system' (De Vries, 1988).

The arguments for this proposition are twofold: the management structures of the "workplace" and the "school" obey to a different logic, and the learning contents are either clearly professional and practical or theoretical and general. The conclusion of the study is not that one better stops working towards an integration, but that there exists a possibility of limited integration under three basic conditions: the "work organisation" and the "school organisation" must each assume their typical educative responsibility, both curricula must be fully worked out and respected in their process and outcomes, and the "student" role must gradually become secondary to the "professional role" of the future worker.

The division between "on-the-job" and "off-the-job" training appears to be too narrow and too limited, even within the framework of vocational/professional education. This is the conclusion of an extensive review of the literature, conducted by K. Prosmans in preparation of an evaluation of the apprenticeship system of trades and commerce in Belgium (Prosmans, 1992). Further reflection has generated the overall table of the different forms of education and learning in relationship to work and professional functioning, presented on the next page. We make first of all a distinction between theoretical/general education, which usually takes place in an institutional setting (school, training centre, community centre etc.) and vocational/practical education which can take place in an institutional setting, but very often is realised close to or in the workplace. The arrow from one type of orientation to the other symbolises the possibility of a gradual shift from one to the other. We here add the distinction made earlier between intentional/systematic learning and incidental/spontaneous learning. Within the institutional setting, we encounter two types of intentional learning: *general education* and *vocational education/Training off-the-job*. As we indicate below, the first type has no direct relationship to work, the second one clearly has. In institutions, incidental learning has been called "hidden curriculum", meaning that learners are socialised towards the self-evident but largely hidden norms, values, attitudes, etc. There is, however, a clear difference between the hidden curriculum of general education, referring to general social and cultural norms, and that of vocational education, which is clearly related to norms and role expectations in the professions people are being trained for. The relationship between vocational education in schools and work is ambivalent: the greater part of it takes place in the "school", but part of it is realised in (usually short) periods of apprenticeship. The same ambivalence exists within training-off-the-job, but then in reverse order: the work process is temporarily interrupted for an "external" training period. In both cases however, the accent will be on "theory". Learning in the workplace, which is clearly oriented to the work situation, also takes on two forms: *training-on-the-job*, for which the work process is occasionally interrupted (usually for very short periods),

Table 7: The relationship between education, learning and work

THEORETICAL/GENERAL ORIENTATION ---> VOCATIONAL/PRACTICAL ORIENTATION			
INSTITUTIONAL LEARNING		LEARNING IN THE WORKPLACE	
GENERAL EDUCATION	VOCATIONAL EDUCATION / TRAINING-OFF-THE-JOB	TRAINING - ON-THE-JOB	
HIDDEN CURRICULUM	HIDDEN CURRICULUM	LEARNING-ON-THE-JOB	
no direct orientation to work	occasional work experi-ence/ work process occasionally interrupted	work process occasional-ly interrupted	work process uninter-rupted

and *learning-on-the-job*, which can be compared to the "hidden curriculum" of educational institutions. In former times, the scheme above was realised from left to right: first "general education", then "preparation for work" and then "work-and-some-incidental learning". Nowadays, there is no longer a standard sequence. Furthermore, as we have said, there have been developed systems and programmes which explicitly link institutional education/learning with workplace learning. As we have seen, this attempt to reconcile the culture of the expert with that of the engineer can only be realised in part, and under specific conditions. This means, in other words, that the strengths and the weaknesses of both models and cultures become apparent when efforts are made to combine them in the sphere of education-for-and-in-work. The engineering culture of education is clearly less concerned with general education, the problem of values and of giving meaning to life.

THE CULTURE OF PROPHETIC EDUCATION: THE PILGRIMAGE TO A NEW HEAVEN AND A NEW EARTH

"When shall they ever learn ?" sang one of the bards of the flower-power generation, pondering the Vietnam war, pollution and other calamities of modern times. His question was not about the processing of "new information" or about acquiring new "action skills". His question was about basic values like justice, peace, respect of man and nature, sobriety ... and "all we need is love" as another famous song tells us.

One of the (stereo)typical reactions to crises and disasters in past and present is a call upon the world of education to help remedy or at least prevent such events. Whether it is the atom bomb on Nagasaki, the starving of Africans in Ethiopia, the nuclear explosion of Tsjernobil, the ethnic murderings in Sarajevo or the epidemic of Aids, the public voice demands a humanitarian vision and positive values to be instilled and/or corroborated by educational measures. This is a call on the prophet-educator to go to his people and hold up the Table with the ten commandments like Moses did, and show the people the way to liberation.

But shall the people learn? History of prophetic action - be it that of ancient times - with the classical examples of Hesiod and Socrates in Greece and of religious prophets like Amos, Jeremiah, Mohammed or Jesus himself - or that of modern times, incorporated e.g. by Mahatma Gandhi, Martin Luther King and the authors of Charta 77 in Czechoslovakia - tells us that the recipients of their messages not only failed to learn from them in most cases, but often stilled the prophetic voices through personal or structural violence. The cantico "I have a dream" was still resounding over cities and villages of the United States, when M. Luther King was shot dead.

Here, we immediately come upon the basic dilemma of prophecy in general and of prophetic education in particular: the message which people seem to wait for, is often repudiated as quickly as it is pronounced. This is at least the conclusion drawn by D. Deshler in his analysis of the relationship between prophecy, adult education and the politics of power: 'Throughout Judeo-Christian history, the prophets have been those who have stood for justice and proclaimed it, at whatever the personal cost. This proclamation has usually not been welcomed within the ranks of either politics or religion, let alone the educational establishment. While prophets have drawn their critical perspectives from religious traditions, they have been persecuted by their own religious establishments as well as by their contemporary political, economic and often educational power structures. Religious prophetic voices are often in leadership positions within social movements, bringing theological and ideological dimensions to social action' (Deshler, 1992, p. 273)

It would be wrong, however, to link the culture of prophetic education exclusively to religious movements or to the churches. Some of the great revolutions of modern times - the French and the Russian notably - were not calling upon God or religion - and the reason for this was not simply their rejection of the corruptive practices and the elitist attitudes of the different christian churches. Next to brotherhood, solidarity and justice, they also proclaimed human liberty and freedom, and initially some of their leaders also acted according to those values. Besides royalty and the first or upper class, one of their prime action targets was the existing educational establishment. Thus, the Russian communists initiated the first historic example of a "Death of the School" movement, proclaiming that school education ought to be liberated from its alienation from society and brought back again to the world of labour and social practice, in a kind of praxis-oriented "project education in the workplace". (Van Moen, 1984)

A most inspiring example of a prophetic view on education has been given by one of the intellectual leaders of the French Revolution, namely M.J.A. Condorcet. It is only recently that his unique position and leadership has been fully recognised, through an extensive in-depth historical analysis made by I. and R. Badinter, a rare example of scholarship-for-the people, which has received a warm response. (Badinter, 1988, 1991)

On April 20th 1792, Condorcet presented his 'Report and project about the general organisation of public instruction', a carefully constructed plea for a total reorganisation of what he called 'instruction' or school education, starting with a central observation:

'We have indeed observed that instruction does not have to abandon individuals at the moment when they leave the school; that this instruction has to embrace all ages; that there is no age at which it would be useless or impossible to learn, and that this second instruction is all the more necessary, given the fact that the first one has been entrenched within narrow bounds' (our transl.). This is, in fact, the first public declaration on lifelong learning, stressing the need for an educational system that would embrace all ages and all social classes. (Cacéres, 1964) However, there is more to it. First of all, Condorcet criticised the rationalistic and fragmented nature of school education, pleading for a system which would 'embrace the complete system of human knowledge' and allow people to 'conserve' or even 'enlarge' their ability to learn. This makes it one of the first, though fairly general, playdoyers for a system of what has been called later comprehensive education. Secondly, Condorcet does not found his reform proposal on the needs of the state or of the revolution, but on a set of ethical principles. Right at the start of his report, he formulates the aims of a system of 'public instruction': 'to offer, to all members of the human race, the means to fulfil their needs, to assure their well-being, to know and execute their rights, ...

and thus, to create among the citizens a factual equality of opportunities and, in so doing, realise the political equality which they have been awarded' (our transl.) This is indeed an educational translation of the three major principles of the French Revolution. It is interesting to note that Condorcet, who had suffered under an extremely severe and indoctrinating jesuitic education, refuted any subservience of the school to any single religion or ideology. Condorcet's report had also a very practical side: he proposes to set up a system of 'écoles du dimanche' or Sunday schools, where the headmaster of the local school would lecture, i.a. about the moral principles and the rights and duties of citizens. This idea would only be realised 40 years later, under the ministry of Guizot.

The voice of the prophet Condorcet was heard, but not followed by the revolutionary assembly. And one year later, that voice was stilled forever, when, not surprisingly, Condorcet spoke out against the Jacobinean violence and the death of King Louis XVII, clashed with Robespierre, and was put into jail where he died.

There seem to be periods when the voice of prophets or prophetic movements is clearly heard and responded to, and other periods when "they are calling in the desert". The second half of the 19th century in Europe seemed to be such a fruitful prophetic period, with the rise of workers' movements and the messages, first, of Karl Marx, and then of the churches, leading to the founding of labour unions and workers' parties, who in turn, provoked the introduction of new rights at the beginning of the 20th century - such as the right for every citizen (man or woman) to vote - and the instalment of compulsory school systems open to all children of the nation-state. Hand in hand with these movements - and often rather as a complement than as an initiator - educational institutions were created: the People's Universities in Italy, Belgium and the Netherlands, the German Arbeiterbund and its workers' clubs, N. Grundtvigs "Fölkelig Hojskule" or "Folk High School" in Denmark and its residential courses for young adults, The Workers' Educational Association in Great Britain and its tutored courses, J. Cardijn's Young Christian Workers' Movement and its method of "Seeing, Judging and Acting" in Belgium, and later in the whole of Europe and in other continents.

Another such prophecy-prone period seemed to be the second half of the 1960s and the beginning of the '70s. That period has been called by some "the second great emancipatory wave", after the first one of the second half of the 19th century. In that period, several "liberation" movements seemed to unfold like leaves of one great flower: students' rebellion from "the Free Speech movement" in California to "the movement of May '68 in France and Germany", anti-authoritarian education, the (second) Death of the School movement of Illich and the Cuernavaca-group, the "conscientisaçao" literacy education movement lead by P. Freire in Brasil and spreading throughout Latin America, the German trade union education programmes following O. Negt's "exemplary learning", the American Civil Rights movement, the citizenship schools and workers' action programmes of M. Horton's Highlander Folk School in Tennessee.

Several of these movements and educational actions have been described and analyzed by such authors as Lovett (Lovett, 1988), Von Hentig (Von Hentig, 1975) and Jarvis (Jarvis, 1982).

Where did this " multiple liberation movement" take its roots? Some state that the end of "the golden sixties", or, in economic parlance, the downward slope of the third Kondratyeff cycle, played a decisive role. Others point to the virtual end of "modernist culture" and the "rise of a youth generation which had lost their parents belief in the state and the market" as a major cause. Let us just remember that no major scientific voice had prognosticated the movement. On the contrary, a French sociological youth report spoke of 'an orderly youth generation, with only some violent "groupuscules" trying to sow unrest' (Jousselin, 1966), and another study based on hundreds of interviews with 14-16 year olds spoke of a "soft, realistic and gentle generation" (Cammaer, 1967). And it was only in 1972 that the concerns signalled by the environmental, the third World and the peace movements were translated into a much-debated scientific study published by the "Club of Rome" under the title: *Limits to growth.* (Meadows e.a., 1972)

The powers of prophecy are not restricted to movements and educational programmes: they also extend to educational theory and research. This applies to the so-called second wave of emancipation as well. Let us look at two examples, which were clearly linked to some of the social movements and educational practices evoked above: German "Emanzipatorische Pädagogik" or emancipatory pedagogy, and P. Freires "Pedagogía del Oprimido" or Pedagogy of the Oppressed.

The term *emancipation* has in fact a long history, and goes back to classic Roman times, where "e-mancipatio" was a ritual act performed by the "pater familias" or the head of the family, who, by laying his hands on the head of his young son, set him free from the "mancipium" of paternal power, endowing him with the capacity to exert his full rights and perform his duties as a free citizen. From the onset, emancipation was thus linked to personal and political autonomy. As we know, only a restricted elite could gain access to this status. The three great modern revolutions - the english "glorious" revolution of 1642, liberating the puritan tradespeople and the gentry from royalty and high nobility, the French Revolution of 1789, setting free the "tiers état" from the dominance of king, church and nobility, and the Russian Revolution of 1917, liberating industrial workers from the tzar and the "bourgeois" upper class - were all efforts to realise a "greater" emancipation for parts of the "under-classes". (Zangerle, 1986)

In educational practice and theory, the notion of "emancipatory learning" and "emancipatory pedagogy" is of very recent origin: it was introduced into the educational debate towards the end of the 1960s. However, its content of learning towards personal and social freedom, had already been enunciated by late Renaissance and early modern writers like de Montaigne, Comenius, Pestalozzi and Kant. In our introduction, we already referred to Kant's concept of *Mündigkeit*, which literally means the ability to act without a custodian. For the first time in history, education became an act of self-liberation, with clear political implications, since it implied a critical stance towards the traditional powers of kings, nobility and churches.

However, between the second and the third "modern" revolution, it became clear that the "enlightened" citizens not only kept the advantages of their emancipation to their private circles, but also subjected workers and, in many cases also farmers, to new forms of industrial or economic slavery. The same sort was imposed on some minority groups like Jews, gypsies and low-educated women. In one of his early writings, *Zur Judenfrage*, Karl Marx discussed the fate of the Jews in the light of the "modern" concept of emancipation. To him, the main question was not "Who shall emancipate ?" and "Who should be emancipated ?", but rather: "What kind of emancipation are we talking about?" In his answer to that question, he opposed what he called "political" to "human" emancipation. The political emancipation of ca 1855 was that of the liberal-industrial society, which officially guaranteed such rights as free choice of religion, education, property etc. but reduced these to the private sphere of the individual and ignored the exploitation of salaried workers. For Karl Marx, "Human emancipation", on the contrary, meant the liberation of all people out of their alienation from their true needs, the dissolution of the opposition between capital and labour, and the integration of the "state citizen" and the "individual person" into the "one, fundamental human being" (das Gattungswesen Mensch), by means of an intermediary class struggle on the road to a classless society.

At the theoretical level, Marx wanted to integrate personal autonomy with collective solidarity, and he expected that a revolution of labour conditions would work the wonder. He had little confidence in the school system or in education in general, because the class struggle and the work floor would be the central learning places.

In his survey of theories of emancipation and emancipatory education, G. Hartfiel opens with the following statement: 'A few centuries of Enlightenment and one hundred years of marxism have, in the light of the real historical evolution, generated strong doubts, as well about the bourgeois belief in progress as about the marxist-socialist interpretation of history as the dynamics of de-alienation" (Hartfiel, 1975, our transl.). The latter statement is broadened to the whole spectrum of classic marxist theory by J. Stalpers : 'For the future, there is no choice. The outcome of the political process has been fixed already, as well as the process which generates it. What will happen is the dialectic lawful transition from exploitation to emancipation... The scientist is the stenographer of Donna Historia who is on her self-sufficient way to the great delivery room.' (Stalpers, 1981, p. 102). What both authors could not suspect at the time they were writing was what would happen some ten years later: the marxist state and the "classic" marxist concept of emancipation may have reached some delivery rooms, but their children nearly all died with the crumbling of the Berlin wall.

Does this mean that emancipation, and its prophetic call to personal and social autonomy, have also become meaningless? Hartfiel himself did not reach that conclusion in his comprehensive and critical study, at least not for those emancipatory concepts and theories which could be situated between the extremes of conservative liberalism and orthodox marxism. He thereby referred especially to three authors: K. Mollenhauer, H. Giesecke and P. Freire. We will deal here with the first and the last one.

With his book *Erziehung und Emanzipation* (Education and emancipation), K. Mollenhauer became the "father" of German emancipatory pedagogy. (Mollenhauer, 1968) He was the only one who clearly defined the concept, situated it in the context of the theories of the Frankfurt School - especially Adorno, Horkheimer and Habermas - and tried to spell out the conditions of a practice of emancipatory education. His definition became the standard reference during the '70s in Germany and the Netherlands: 'Emancipation means the liberation of human subjects - in our case of adolescents in today's society - from conditions which delimit their rationality and their concomitant social action.' (o.c., p. 11)

As one can see, the primary accent is laid on reflexive personal autonomy and rationally founded social action. One could call this a socio-critical position. Its rational overtones - caused also by the fact that education was mainly reduced to school education - were criticised by some authors, like H. Giesecke, who had close ties with "out-of-school" youth and community work, and stressed the importance of starting from real life experiences and trying to create "free spaces" for democratic action. (Giesecke, 1973). The works of authors like Mollenhauer and Giesecke did not merely function as textbooks for "critical students" at German universities, they also provided concepts and criteria for practical school reform, like the experiment of comprehensive secondary education (Gesamtschule) in the province of Hessen. The youth work scene responded fairly actively to Giesecke's proposal for emancipatory youth work, as Becker's study proves (Beckers, h. J., 1982, 1983). At the same time they provoked a strong and sometimes irrational debate between the precited authors on the one hand, and defenders of traditional pedagogy like Brezinka, Rössner and Wilhelm. (Brezinka, 1981; Rössner, 1973; Wilhelm, 1979).

Our second author, Paolo Freire, comes from quite a different background than Mollenhauer's Bundesrepublik Deutschland: he was born and grew up in the Northeastern Brazilian province of Pernambuco, as the oldest son of a military police officer in the capital of Recife. The economic crash of 1933 forced the family to move out to the countryside, and there the lower-middle class boy experienced the fate of extreme poverty, an experience which marked him for the rest of his life. He could nevertheless terminate his secondary education, even though he was far from a brilliant student, who e.g. kept on writing 'ratón' (mouse) with a double 'rr'. Back in Recife, he first studied Law, and became a lawyer at the provincial court. The fact that he, in defending poor campesinos, lost his first cases, made him return to the university and study philosophy and education. After presenting his doctoral dissertation about the educational system, he continued to work out his critical ideas about pedagogy as a professor of education. His earlier experiences with traditional literacy education as the leader of the section for Education and Culture of the "charitative" organisation SESI were now rethought in the light of the psychology of E. Fromm, the existential philosophy of G. Marcel and others, neo-marxist theories like those of L. Althusser and A. Gramsci, M. Buber's dialogical concept of education, and the works of a study group of young Brazilian sociologists and economists.

Within the framework of christian and social organisations, Freire experimented with a revolutionary method of literacy education from 1964 onwards, first with four agricultural workers, and then with larger groups which were called "cultural circles". Gradually it came to a plan for a national campaign in 1965, whereby about 20.000 cultural circles would be set up, following a training programme for literacy educators in the whole of the country. The plan for the 'alphabetization' of about one million illiterates was torpedoed after the military coup of '66 which ousted civil president Goulart. Freire was put in jail and accused of being "a traitor of Jesus and the Brazilian people". He emigrated to Chile, and it was there that "the psycho-social method" was systematically worked out and described. In the case of Freire, theory followed reflexive practice. The first book that caught the attention was a descriptive analysis of this practice: 'Educación como practica de la libertad' or 'Education as the practice of freedom'. (Freire, 1969) It was soon followed by a systematic theoretical foundation : 'Pedagogía del oprimido' or 'Pedagogy of the oppressed', according to several commentators the best book Freire has ever published (Freire, 1970). It was complemented by an essay where the cultural and political aspects received greater attention: 'Cultural action for freedom' (Freire, 1972). The following explanation combines these three sources, complemented by further materials gathered by a former student of his work until 1975 (Hernandez, 1977).

In line with the sources mentioned above, and with his own experience, Freire views the relationship between man and the world as a dialectical one: as historic subject, man is situated within a world which determines him to a certain degree, yet leaves room to change and humanise it. 'In history, in concrete and objective contexts, both humanisation and de-humanisation belong to the possibilities of man, that unfinished being which is conscious of its own shortcomings... only humanisation is the true vocation of man.' (Freire, 1970, p. 47) This humanisation is an intersubjective process, taking on the form of a dialogue. With reference to the Brazilian situation of the 1960s, Freire speaks of a dualistic society, with a small power elite and a large powerless majority which has no voice, and lives in "the culture of silence". Education is simply a reproduction of that situation: in its "banking" tradition, it views students as "bank accounts" where "deposits" are transferred down from above: 'the teacher teaches, the pupil is taught. The teacher knows all, the pupil knows nothing... the teacher is the subject of the learning process, whereas the students are mere objects'. To that banker's concept, he opposes the concept of 'concientisaçao' or conscientisation, a process which starts with the exploration of the 'thematic universe' of the living subjects, especially in its 'frontier situations'. Such situations are not 'border lines separating Being from Non-being', but rather 'the border line which separates Being from potentially Being More', or areas of transformative action.

In the culture of silence, people are immersed in a 'magic' or 'naive' conscience, believing that all things that happen to them or in society 'come from above', are 'God's will'. People can and should be stimulated to reach a 'transitive and critical consciousness'. This is the process of 'conscientisation': 'Conscientisaçao constitutes the transition from a spontaneous to a critical perception of reality, where reality is looked at as an object of true knowledge. Man assumes a position of authentic critical conscience of reality.' In this sense we are touching upon Utopia, not as an illusionary dream, but as an unexplored possibility.

When Freire wrote the statements presented above, he and his teams had already worked out the so-called 'metodo psico-social' to a large extent. Basically, it contains two phases. The first phase is that of the *analysis of the thematic universe* and the *codification of key-situations and key-words*. In short, this means that a multidisciplinary team moves out to live with a certain community for a few months, observes situations, listens to the nature of their communication and gathers typical expressions. Linguists then select 15 - 17 "generative" words, according to their phonemic richness and their socio-cultural and political meaning. These words are illustrated by corresponding existential situations which represent each word in part or as a whole. This process of *codification* ends when the chosen words and situations have been visualised on slides/pictures/posters. The pictures presented below belong to the first series of drawings used in 1964-65 in Pernambuco, and represent the following words: trabajo (work) and cazador (hunter).

The second phase is that of 'alphabetization ' or *literacy education itself*. Let us illustrate the 6-step process with a concrete example, which was quite frequently used: the session around the word *favela,* meaning poor neighbourhood or poor house, as we ourselves also saw it applied on a few occasions.

1) participants are gathered in their cultural circle in a school, house or community centre. The animator welcomes them and announces the presentation of a new "life scene". The picture shown represents a simple hut, a "favela". The participants are asked to tell what they see, and what they connect with the picture (*de-coding*). Some frequent answers are: "this is one of our houses", "we eat there", "our house is different", "this is the place where the family stays", "the cost of life is high"... A brief discussion follows.

2) The word FAVELA is projected or shown together with the picture, and partici-pants start to make the link between word and picture.

3) Now, the word FAVELA is projected/shown separately, and read aloud.

4) The word is partitioned into its syllables, and read: FA-VE-LA. Participants start to identify the separate syllables as phonemes

5) Then the three (in this case) phonemic "families" are shown *separately*, in the alphabetic vowel sequence. The learners start to read them, and thus discover the separate vowels:

Figure 9: Codification for the words 'cultura' and 'cazador' in first literacy programme of Freire's teams

FA - FE - FI - FO - FU

VA - VE - VI - VO - VU

LA - LÉ - LI - LO - LU

6) Finally, the three families are *shown together*, which allows learners to discover the different vowels and the different consonants. The "decisive" moment has now arrived: the "creative discovery" of new words by participants, who are encouraged to form "new words" themselves in written form, by combining different phonemes. Therefore, the slide/poster showing the three syllable families is called 'ficha de discubrimiento' or 'discovery card'. Learners may come up with some of the following combinations: VE-LA (candle), LU-VA (glove), LA-VO (I wash),

VA-LE (valley), VE-LO (hide), etc. At the end of the session of about 2 hours, participants return home with a piece of homework: to "make" new words. This process - a variant of one well-known method - is of course made easier by the monosyllabic character of the Spanish (and somewhat less: the Portuguese) language. The whole series of 15-17 situations and words is worked through in about 20 sessions.

The "method" was a great success. In many cases, participants were able to write their own names at the end of the first session, which had also political implications, since only literate people were allowed to vote. If there came no breakthrough in Brazil - at least not in the mid-sixties - the method was successfully applied in many other latin-american countries: Chile, Peru, Venezuela, Mexico. The most spectacular success was reached in Nicaragua during the famous "Crusade" of 1980-1981 after the Somoza-regime was overthrown by the Sandinistas - even though P. Freire was never directly involved in its preparation. In about 4 years, the Nicaraguan illiteracy rate was reduced with 35 %! (Salgado, 1984, Salgado & Leirman, 1985). In the second half of the '70s, P. Freire became the most famous educator-in-exile, the bearded prophet of conscientisation and cultural action for freedom, who cooperated from his World Council of Churches base in Geneva with Latin American, European and African countries. Our own university of Leuven awarded him a doctorate honoris causa in 1975. On that occasion, he gave an acceptance speech, in which he stated that the honour did not befall on him but on his latin-american campesinos. At the same time, he failed to grasp the opportunity to share some of his deep thoughts on education with an academic audience which was, to 90%, composed of members of other disciplines.

On the whole, however, the promise of "liberation through conscientisation"
- promulgated by several movements, church organisations and even some governments in Latin-America - was not fulfilled: the outspoken intention of the 1985 Declaration of Mexico to "eradicate illiteracy before the year 2000" seems to be an unattainable target. The combined group of ministers of education and of economy assembled there made a complex and rather unusual multiple analysis of the causes of illiteracy: poverty, economic crisis, lack of democracy, shortcomings of the traditional school systems, discrimination against ethnic groups, lack of trained educators and adequate materials... By doing so, they may themselves have provided arguments for those who termed the eradication declaration as "illusionary rhetoric". In some cases, the "psycho-social method" was stripped of its prophetic conscientisation content - like in Mexico, where the National Institute for Adult Education used the method as a mere didactic instrument - avoiding any kind of critical group discussion.

Like several other departments of social pedagogy and adult education, we ourselves got strongly involved in the emancipatory debate during the '70s, in at least two ways. First of all, there were student actions in favour of the introduction of project work as a central part of the study programme. The project method - worked out in the 1920s in the USA under the inspiring leadership of Dewey and Kirpatrick - now became a "weapon in the hands of the student movement to reform the educational system" in hundreds of secondary schools and universities in Europe. After two years of experimenting and confrontational discussions, we indeed implemented a kind of intensive project work, based on a "blueprint" where "emancipatory educational science" was delineated as an effort to combine three criteria: truth, well-being and methodical-practical usefulness.

Secondly, we were engaged in several research projects under the umbrella of emancipation. In 1974, we joined an empirical study into the "degree of emancipation of Dutch and Flemish youngsters", under the supervision of the Hoogveld institute, and let it follow by action research projects in Flanders and (West-)Germany. (Welten, 1973; Verbeke, 1977; Beckers, 1982).

Within the framework of this project, we construed a synthetic definition of emancipation based upon an extensive literature survey: 'emancipation is the process whereby individuals develop a critical consciousness of and a socio-emotional reaction to hindersome socially determined dependencies and try to work out liberating alternatives; this process involves both rationality, emotion and action'. We also developed a theory of "youth emancipation" with 13 propositions, centred around the critical variables of "readiness c.q. the realised potential to participate in decisions which have a bearing on the life orientation of youngsters". The statistical analysis of about 200 interviews allowed us to construct 62 Gutman scales and to state that *readiness to participate in life-orienting decisions* was positively correlated with such variables as self-esteem, high social aspiration, personal autonomy, orientation towards actual or critical information in the media, a proclivity to social care and social action, readiness to engage in open contact with adult peers (Leirman, 1977)...
At the same time, we found out that in the three national samples, the wish to participate was significantly greater than the degree of realisation in the life spheres of the family, the school, the workplace and youth work.

In our previous chapter, we pointed to the methodological switch from empirical-analytical to action-oriented research under the impulse of the engineering culture of education. The same trend was continued in the "emancipatory decade of the '70s", and that in many areas of the human sciences. However, the arguments underpinning this option were different from those given by the "engineers of change". The accent was put on the "discursive nature" of action-oriented research, stating that researchers had to listen first to their partners in the practice fields and engage in a dialogue, as Moser argued in his book on action research in the social sciences (Moser, 1975). With many other, especially Latin-american authors, Hall spoke of *participatory research*, meaning that dialogical education and dialogical research had to be linked together, in order to give participants the opportunity to become the authors of their own change process. (Hall, 1975)

Our second 'emancipatory' research project clearly stood in this participatory line. In 1977 we were approached from two sides to engage ourselves in a "type of action research" for a local neighbourhood organisation. Leaders of the community centre "The little Lamp" asked us to help them develop "the educative function" of their

Table 7: Design of the project "Creativity and Emancipation in the Neighbourhood (KREMAB, 1977 - 1982)

DIAGNOSIS OF NEIGHBOURHOOD LIFE			INHABITANTS' GROUPS BUILDING EXECUTION		EVALU-ATION OF RESULTS
100 INTER-VIEWS AT HOME VALIDITY CHECK OF MAJOR CONTENTS WITH INTER-VIEWEES	CONTENT ANALYSIS OF THE INTER-VIEWS 8 CENTRAL THEMES (i.a. Work, education, family life)	ANIMATED EXHIBI-TION about 8 CENTRAL THEMES 356 VISI-TORS INVITA-TION TO PARTICI-PATE IN INHABI-TANTS' GROUPS	BI-WEEKLY NEIGHBOUR-HOOD MEAL (± 25 par-ticipants) HOUSING GROUP (± 12 par-ticipants) └─>	IDEM HOUSE RENOVA-TION GROUP	CELE-BRATION COMMIT-TEE PRESEN-TATION OF RE-NOVA-TION PLAN TO CITY COUNCIL

APR. '77	-	OCT. '78	JAN. '79 - APR. '79	OCT. 1979	-	APR. 1981

practical work, which had been thus far basically oriented to social assistance. And the ministry of culture wanted to set up common projects for the "promotion of creativity of the ordinary citizen"

The confluence of these two requests lead to a project called 'Creativity and Emancipation in the Neighbourhood' shortened to KREMAB, which started in 1977 and ended in 1981. We made a contract with the Community Centre which was operating in an underprivileged neighbourhood in the northwest of the town of Leuven, with about 2800 inhabitants. The team of four researchers and two social workers worked out a mission statement with two general goals:

- to offer inhabitants of a so-called "underprivileged" community the opportunity to express their life experiences, their problems and their expectations among themselves and to the local authorities;

- to develop projects together with them in order to better the quality of their lives and their situation.

The statement also contained a paragraph on the mutual engagement of researchers and practitioners. The latter were clearly suspicious that the "people form the university" would only play the role of critical observers, without really cooperating with them as true neighbourhood workers.

The two-phase design, developed in the "P.O.M"-project described in the precious chapter was used here again, although with some important variations, which were the fruit of long discussions. We show the (final) design in the figure on the next page. Given the fact that neither the social workers nor the researchers had a sufficient knowledge of the neighbourhood, we started again with a "diagnosis". This time, however, it differed both in content and process from the previous project. We realised 100 interviews in the homes of a randomly selected group of inhabitants, in which we formulated a single major question: "You have been living here for quite some years. We would like to hear from you what living in this neighbourhood means to you ?" At the same time, we explained the nature of the planned project, and announced a future exhibit in a nearby former grammar school, where the results of our "home visits" would be shown. We saw to it that all streets were reasonably well represented, and that the people visited belonged to the middle-lower and lower classes.

The interview material, mostly registered by the interviewers after the visit - since most inhabitants did not permit us to tape-record what they said - was content-analyzed, and reduced to a number of *central themes*. We then went back with this result to the interviewees, and let them decide whether we had "understood them in the right way". In a second, global analysis, we reduced the whole material to 8 central themes, from "Labour/work" and "Education" to "Urbanisation" and "Health/Hygiene". We then "encoded" these contents into drawings, pictures, popular sayings and quotations. Exactly 356 of the 2.800 inhabitants visited the "animated exhibit" on a cold weekend of January 1979. We also provided a "talking corner" and a popular pub, so that visitors could meet their neighbours and the organisers. At the same time, we invited visitors to participate in so-called "inhabitants groups" where some of the themes could be further discussed and acted on. The result was limited. In the following months, we were able to start two groups only: a slightly reformed "neighbourhood meal group" which was meeting every two weeks in the centre for a self-prepared meal, and a "housing group", which would tackle the problem of deterioration of old houses and possibly work out a renovation project. The two groups knew different structures and employed different methods. In the "neighbourhood meal group" the focus was on pleasant contacts and on cultivating the popular kitchen, and the "facilitators" restricted themselves to observing participation patterns, and to organising an "after-dinner talk". The secret hope was that some participants would volunteer to work in the neighbourhood organisation, and that happened indeed, for the aspect "organisation of neighbourhood festivities".

In the housing group, the two facilitators, one architect and one educator, wanted - in freirean terms - to "problematicize" the lamentable state of many houses, and they did so by letting the inhabitants make pictures of their homes and the street environment, and then inviting them to "decode" the pictures. This process was far from easy, and only under the influence of the facilitators, did the group prepare a set of proposals to be made to the city urbanisation service. Nevertheless, they became the first neighbourhood to receive a firm renovation subsidy from the Flemish ministry.

Thinking back on the large project goals enounced above, we could only come to the conclusion that the results, after four years of work, were really limited. The major results were in fact the reorganisation of the neighbourhood centre itself, the development of a functional theory of community work and of a number of methods for future practice, like "home visits/interviews" and "animated exhibition". The "self-organisation of the inhabitants" did not come about. The prophetic message "become conscious of your underprivileged situation and take your own sort in your own hands" was only heard and applied by a few. On the other hand, when student project groups went back to work in youth work and training-for-renovation projects some 6 to 8 years later, they found a neighbourhood organisation which was far stronger than at the time of our project, and could count on a somewhat greater participation of inhabitants.

The clash between high expectations and limited results should not wonder, in the light of what happened elsewhere. In 1981, an international colloquy was held in Brussels on the future of the human sciences. In one section, the theme of discussion was "action research and its theoretical and practical implications". The analysis of some 20 projects realised in different sectors proved that "research in order to emancipate" had remained by and large a dream. Several participants tended to impute the lack of results to the socio-economic crisis of the late '70s, to the crisis of the "welfare state" and to the lack of adequate strategies and methods. Our own team rather thought that "our emancipation and theirs" did not quite coincide, and that some important practical and theoretical results had been obtained nevertheless. (Leirman e.a. 1982)

The examples given above all resort to the area of adult education and community work. Would that be the preferential soil for the seeds of prophecy? A contemporary as well as a historical analysis leads to a far more nuanced conclusion. In the '60s and '70s, several large and small experiments of "emancipatory education" were set up in the area of primary, secondary and higher education: "anti-authoritarian" schools in Great Britain, West-Germany and the Netherlands, the revival of the Freinet-type schools in Belgium and the Netherlands, the introduction of project work as basic method for a whole school system or even - as in the case of Roskilde in Denmark - for a whole university, and - above all - the attempts to develop a comprehensive secondary school system in countries like Sweden and Germany.

In the previous chapter, we evoked the three professional school cultures detected by K. Staessens in her study of the application of the VLO-innovation project for grammar schools: the "family school", the "professional school" and the "living-apart-together school". Throughout the whole study, we barely find any clear reference to a "prophetic" culture. That may well be a "significant blind spot", not of the study, but of the 1990s, especially when we compare it to historical periods and traditions of school education. Th. Ballauff repeatedly describes the "condition of confessionality" in the evolution of schools and the teaching profession. By confession, he not only means 'the great christian confessions, not only the religious orientations labelled as "sects", but also all other religions with their many variants, e.g. Islam with Sunites and Shiites' (Ballauff, o.c., p. 49 f.). Among the "christian" examples, the author quotes the Jesuitic *Ratio atque Insititutio Studiorum Societas Jesu*, edited in Naples in 1559:

"1. The boys, who have been submitted to our society for their education, must be taught by the teacher in such a way, that they, together with the sciences, acquire the worthy behaviour of a christian...

6. Even if there is no threat to faith or piety, nobody should introduce new questions or new opinions... without prior consultation of the authorities... One should rather follow the traditional teachers and teachings, which have been accepted after long years of experience in catholic academies.."

For centuries, and down into our period, the order of St. Ignatius has followed this teaching path. Our impression about the present situation, however, is that jesuitic education reflects the religious, ethical and social pluralism which one encounters in all christian churches.

In the last decades of the 20th century, we may better direct our search for religiously inspired prophetic education to the islamitic world. Looking at a comparative study of youth education in Egypt and Iraq between 1920 and 1980, the reader can only conclude that the Islam, in both its Sunite and Shiite versions, has basically conserved the tradition of koranic education which started in the first century of Islam (Al Kasey, 1984). During the Abasside period in Iraq (750 - 1258), three main educational institutions were created: the *Kuttab* or *Maktab*, i.e. the "writing" school at private teachers' homes, the *Masjid* or *Mosque* school and the *Madrasah*, which came to replace the two former institutions by way of state intervention in 1057 a.D. They all were basically oriented at teaching the Koran, islamic theology and islamic law: 'For the first time in the history of Muslim education, the new institutions belonged to the state. The most famous Madrasah, which in time became the model for the whole system, was founded in 1057 by the Nizam-Al-Mulk in Bagdad known as Al-Nizamyah. The principle motive was ... religious. Its objective was the teaching of the "shafiite school of law", its sole emphasis being upon the teaching of theology and Islamic law.' (Al Kasey, o.c. p. 32) In Egypt, the most influential of all educational institutions was *Al-Azhar*, which 'had for centuries developed the feeling that it was responsible for upholding the doctrines of the faith against any encroachment of modern society. With the advent of the twentieth century, Al-Azhar seemed to have exercised an even more important and profound influence on Egyptian mentality than ever before.' (O.c. p. 489)

The author does point to the influences of French and British colonisation, which brought about a "secularisation" in Iraq, but on the other hand, he avoids a reference to the counter-movement of islamic fundamentalism, a movement initiated by Khomeiny in neighbouring Iran. Immigration to the West has confronted several western societies with both the koranic educational tradition and with fundamentalist tendencies.

The foregoing analysis and the concrete illustrations allow us to delineate the contours of what we call the prophetic culture of education and learning. The image of man and society underlying prophetic education is that of *homo viator* or, as we would prefer to say, *homo peregrinus*, the wayfaring human being in search of guiding values and normative orientations. Concurrently, society is seen here as a *moral community* bound by ethical norms and specific action rules, and ultimately by the perspective of liberation from the limitations of the present world: 'Then I saw a new heaven and a new earth: for the first heaven and the first earth had passed away, and the sea was no more. And I saw the holy city, the new Jerusalem, coming down from heaven, from God, prepared as a bride adorned for her husband; and I heard a great voice from the throne saying: "Behold the dwelling of God is with men"... he will wipe away every tear from their eyes, and death shall be no more... And he who sat upon the throne said: "Behold, I make all things new" (Revelation of John, 21: 1 - 5a). The final mission of prophetic education is to prepare people for this ultimate perspective of the moral community, by providing or stimulating ethical values like justice, equality, solidarity, freedom. As was said above, this involves some kind of utopia. Mannheim states that there are four different types of utopian mentality:

- the orgiastic chiliasm of the Anabaptists, believing in the expression or effusion of the divine spirit through man;
- the humanitarian liberalism of e.g. the French revolution;
- the conservative idea, which sees individual property as the basis of morality;
- the socialist-communist utopia, which, on the contrary, sees the abolishment of property and individualism as the ultimate remedy to the problems of mankind. (in: Jarvis, 1992, p. 314 f.)

Whatever kind of utopia is adopted, the kind of learning involved on the way to adopt it can be termed as *value transmission*, c.q. *value clarification*. (Scientia Pedagogica experimentalis, 1988,). One could also say that the process of learning here is one of "learning after a moral model", which may be represented by a Holy Book, a small community or - indeed - a "charismatic" leader. The power base for the prophetic educator does not reside in the first place in expertise or in a legitimate position, but in his/her charisma and in the learner's identification with the moral model. Therefore, the prophetic culture of education and learning stresses, as we have heard a few times in our examples, the moral integrity of educators: the virtues of the educator are more important than his or her knowledge or skills. He or she will often exhort, "preach", "problematisize".

The basic strategy followed in prophetic education has been termed "normativereeducative" (Bennis e.a., 1967) or "strategy of conscientisation". Its true nature is confrontational: the present situation is analyzed, not only from the viewpoint of experience, but also from the viewpoint of explicit or implicit values and norms: "SEIN" is compared to "SOLLEN", with the expectation that learners will embark upon action to narrow the gap between the two. This action can either consist in "personal conversion", in an attempt at "organisational or structural change" or in a combination of both.

A very interesting example of this strategic orientation is offered by the work of J. Mezirow, who gradually developed a theory of (adult) education as value-lead transformative action. Applying the theory of "knowledge-guiding interests" ("er-kenntnisleitende Interessen") of the younger Habermas (Habermas, 1968) to his empirical analysis of the learning process of women returning to college after years of family and professional life, he developed a theory of *perspective transformation*. Learning is seen here as a change in meaning structures. These structures function as a lens or filter through which experience is captured and interpreted. Experiences passing through this lens may be of two kinds: they may be more or less congruent with past experiences or, on the contrary, present a "disorienting dilemma", a kind of shock. In the first case, they simply reinforce the existing meaning structure, and nothing much is "learned". In the second case, they may either be rejected or cause the formation of a new meaning structure. This process of perspective transformation leads to greater autonomy and responsibility of the person, and is linked to Haber-mas' third so-called knowledge interest, namely the emancipatory or critically reflexi-ve one. (Mezirow, 1975, 1981) Later on, Mezirow stated that 'the purpose of learning is to enable us to understand the meaning of our experiences and to realize values in our lives' (1985, p. 17) He went on to circumscribe the transition from older or uncritically accepted values to new ones as: 'the process of becoming critically aware of how and why the structure of our psychocultural assumptions has come to constrain the way in which we perceive our world, of reconstituting that structure in a way that allows us to be more inclusive and discriminating in our integration of experience and to act on these new understandings' (Mezirow, 1985, p. 22)

This definition comes really close to the definitions of German emancipatory pedagogy: education is a process of liberating oneself from psychocultural constraints and becoming both more autonomous and more critical of society. Mezirow's positioning in fact meant a rupture with the mainstream of North-American adult education, which had kept on stressing maximal self-actualization, professional promotion and consumerism ("learning for the good life"). Looking at Mannheim's four utopian concepts, one could also say that Mezirow's implicit utopia is in line with the idea of 'humanitarian liberalism': all citizens are called upon to become more fully autonomous, more respectful of others and more endowed with democratic rights.

Nevertheless, there is a set of key expressions, which, in the practice and the literature on education and learning from the late 60s to the present day, kept coming back in several variants, and which was often left undefined or was being used in mythological ways: "understanding the meaning of experience", "experiential learning", "exemplary learning"....

As a team of researchers and educators, we did our own pilgrimages through lots of fields and practices. Practitioners often warned us that they adhered to a concept of "experiential learning", which they had filled in "in accordance to their situation and the needs of their participants". The message was sometimes clad in prophetic terms, or underscored by references to Freire, Negt, Illich, Perls. When we kept asking what they meant by "experiential learning", we often received illusive or incomplete answers, which, nevertheless, allowed us to discern several definitions and/or "theories in use".

A very common definition can be phrased as follows: experiential learning is learning on the basis of the experiences of participants. Experiences have to be "thematised", either for their own sake, or, for the sake of illustration of what educators have prepared on beforehand. One could call this the "didactic" definition. We saw it applied in the Cognitively Guided Instruction of mathematics with first grade children in the first chapter, or in the decodation part of freirian literacy education.

A second definition is linked to the first one, but bears ideal/ideological overtones: experiences have to be explored by learners so that they, in a second move, can start to grasp their "real" meaning and implications. That real meaning is related to a framework known to the educators and sometimes also to the participants. Freire's framework is that of the dualism "oppressor/oppressed" and of "conscientisation/cultural action for freedom". Negt's framework is that of neocapitalism, alienation and co-ownership of production means by workers (Negt, 1975). Perls' framework is that of the individual functioning as a fully integrated person independent of all others (Perls, 1968). One could call this the "prophetic" definition, which contains at least two different orientations, depending on the "leading utopia" behind it: an orientation to individual autonomy, and an orientation to communal solidarity.

The nature of the third definition is clearly social-technological and action-oriented : experiential learning is learning from ongoing or newly initiated experiences set up to bring about personal or structural change. Traditionally one speaks of "learning-by-doing". This concept is clearly linked to the engineering approach to education. Some of our interlocutors sated that this was what they aimed at, whereas observation of the real learning process sometimes proved that the definition-in-use was the "didactic" one.

We finally also met a concept that excludes any pre-established goal orientation: "let us look at our experiences in the here and now, communicate about them, and see whether we can learn something from them". It was applied e.g. in some forms of group work, like "Sensitivity training" or "Gestalt" in the 60s and 70s, with a great stress on "total personal growth", the subconscious and non-rational layers of the human personality, and non-verbal forms of communication.

Our inductive exploration of concepts and definitions-in-use leads to the conclusion that "experiential learning" is a "container concept" covering different and often vague notions and practices. This is also the starting point of a recent reader on *adult education, experiential learning and social change.* (Wildemeersch & Jansen, 1992) In the introduction, the authors point to this ambiguity, and the interesting effort at clarification made by Weil and McGill, who distinguish four "villages" of experiential learning:

(1) the assessment and accreditation of experiential learning as an alternative approach to traditional procedures;

(2) the realisation and organisation of institutional change;

(3) conscientisation and community action on the basis of learner's experiences;

(4) personal growth and development (Weil & Mc Gill, 1989).

Even though we are not going deeper into this analysis, it is clear that there is a high degree of convergence between the four "villages" and our "inductive analysis" of four definitions-in-use. Weil e.a. provide a general and broad definition of experiential learning as 'the process whereby people, individually and in association with others, engage in direct encounter and then *purposefully* reflect upon, validate, transform, give personal meaning to and seek to integrate their different ways of knowing' (o.c. p. 248).

However encompassing this definition may be, it leaves two problems unanswered. The first one is presented in great depth by two authors who confront the "theory" of experiential learning represented e.g. in the above definition, with the actual crisis of modernity. (Jansen & Klercq, 1992)

On the one hand, modernity has lead to *fragmentation* of a world which seemed to be unified before around ideologies, market systems, classes and families: "all that is solid melts in the air". Experiential learning as the construction of personal meaning meets very well this postmodern condition: everyone can discover, through confrontation with other experiences, his or her own "truth". But the post-modern world is characterised, at the same time, by *globalisation*. The metaphor of the "Global village" is a fairly apt symbol for the following dimensions indicated by Giddens: a neo-capitalist world economy, the international division of labour, the nation-state and the world military order (Giddens, 1990). We saw at least three of these at work in the Gulf War. But, according to Jansen e.a., none of these dimensions is clearly represented in the "theory" and the practices of experiential learning. They therefore plead for a "meta-theoretical" complement: the adequate use of global theoretical concepts by knowledgeable educators, so that learners can look beyond the narrow limits of their experiences. We will come back to this viewpoint in our next chapter. However, the prophetic version of experiential learning does offer "global frameworks" to participants, but they are "value-oriented", and post-modern man seems to reject any pre-established value orientation, and even doubts the existence of such leading values.

There is a second problem inherent to the bulk of the literature about experiential learning: it fails to give a definition of experience itself! This omission may well be related to the plurality of notions and concepts of experiential learning. It is as if this problem of plurality is tacitly solved by referring to experience itself as a fixed and unified concept. Looking at the literature, one encounters indeed several concepts of experience. One of the first authors to use and define the concept was J. Dewey (Dewey, 1938). He used a metaphor for learning as the exploration of a landscape by a wanderer, and defined experience as our way of *exploring and participating in the world*. The metaphor makes clear that this is a complex process, but nevertheless a straightforward one: the wanderer gets to know the landscape as he moves through it. As C. Clark remarks, there is a problem with this understanding of experience: 'That problematic lies within the nature of subjectivity; we must think about our experience before it can be "ours", yet our thought is not purely our own, but is shaped by language and culture, both of which are socially constructed'. The author gives the example of how the same so-called experience of "sin" and "virtue" in many religions does receive a different meaning, depending on whether it is seen from the perspective of men as opposed to that of women: 'Sin is thus defined as the act of self-assertion at the expense of others; virtue is defined as self-giving love. These are the constructs of the dominant male culture. But women have an innate sense, not of separation, but of connectedness... women are diminished by selflessness, where they can lose their identity in service to others, and expanded by self-assertion, through which they can redress the balance and extend care to themselves' (Clark, 1992). Although one might criticise this interpretation, as did e.g. some groups of housewives participating in our P.O.M-project described above, the example makes it very clear that experience is *mediated and, at least partly, determined by language and culture*.

This leads to a broader concept of experience as a process of exploring dimensions of oneself and the world through the lens of a given language and a given culture. In a sense then, experience is both unique, i.e. personally and historically situated, and at the same time communal, since it can be communicated to and (partially) shared with others. This also implies that one can "learn from the experiences of others", without having gone through them oneself. Furthermore, there is no end to experiencing, and there is no ultimate experience - except maybe the experience of death, which cannot be mediated any more.

At the beginning of this chapter, we quoted Deshler, who made a link between prophecy and social movements. One of the so-called new social movements emerging in the 60s and 70s was the Third World Movement, in which loosely organised groups of people mobilised around the issue of the Development of the so-called Third World and wanted to sensitise the western governments for a new development policy and/or to promote processes of "people-centred development" in the Third World itself. De Aguirre, who, in her study of the peace movement of the

1980s, made an extensive review of the literature on social movements, did not find an inclusive definition, but was able to indicate a number of basic characteristics, such as orientation at public issues or conflicts, stressing of certain "alternative" values, creative use of action methods, intersubjective communication, a specific type of actors (rather young, rather well-educated), inner differences and tensions, gradual transition from anti-hierarchical structure to institutionalisation, learning opportunities. (De Aguirre, 1989)

The Third World Movement opposed the western growth" or *modernisation model*, to either *the basic needs model* or the *New Industrial and Economic Order*. In the growth model, capital, knowledge and technology ought to be transferred from the West to the developing countries with a clear dominance of the "centre" over the "periphery" both "here" and "there" (Galtung, 1973). In the alternative models, one propounds to abolish the North-South rift, either by fulfilling the basic needs of the population for education, health, food and labour, or by reversing the economic power scale and providing the developing countries with better trade opportunities, paying an "honest" price for raw materials, and strongly reducing the debts of the Third World. In an opinion research among leaders and participants of development education programmes, a group of our students found three factors: GROWTH, SELF-INTEREST, STRUCTURAL CHANGE. We take a typical item illustrating each of these :

GROWTH: *'When we talk about development, the developing countries should first listen to us. We have realised a whole process of development, and they can learn from our experiences'*

SELF-INTEREST: *'Preference ought to be given to that kind of development aid which offers contracts to western industry'*

STRUCTURAL CHANGE: *'The actual world trade and economic system should be reformed, because it maintains the inequality between North and South'*

(Dewilde, Jonniaux & Lombaert, 1992)

Most Non-Governmental Organisations working in the Third World can be situated either at the "structural" or at the "basic needs" pole of development concepts. The same can be said of autochthonous movements working "at the popular baseline". Such an organisation is the so-called Andhra Pradesh Social Services Society (APSSS), working in the eastern part of the central Indian state of Andhra Pradesh. Its origins date back to 1976, when the Andhra Pradesh Bishops Council thought of setting up a "Development Apostolate". Almost immediately, the charitative concept of "spending money for the poor" was replaced by a "conscientisation concept" based on Freire's ideas. Development was seen as "the process of self-awareness by which a community raises itself to a more human and responsible way of life; and the process of social liberation that changes those social structures that oppress the poor" (Ambroise, 1992)

The author, one of the pioneers of the organisation, detects two major phases in its short history: a phase of orientation to conscientisation and literacy, and one of "going beyond Paolo Freire" i.e. "towards a just society". In the first phase, the theory and methodology of Freire were "adapted for Andhra Pradesh" via a seminar and a book called "Let my Country awake", in fact part of a poem by Rabindranath Tagore (Pillai, 1979). Following the training of regional supervisors and local facilitators, a total of 295 local centres were set up by APSSS, aiming at the adapted form of literacy education with groups of landless labourers. In the light of some problems and questions, like the reduction to about 190 centres and the small success of exemplary "Pragati Kendras" or "progressive centres", an empirical evaluation of a representative sample of instructors, participants and non-participants was carried out in 1983, which lead to a report in 1985. It stated that APSSS had "succeeded in raising the level of consciousness as measured on 5 dimensions", that the learners had "participated in many constructive activities that ensured a better future for them as well as built up a positive self-image among them". At the same time, the literacy programme appeared to be only partially successful, since "the learners did not immediately see the need of acquiring literacy till they were involved in various negotiations with government and other agencies". This evaluation lead to a revision of the entire APSSS-approach: less attention to small-level issues and individual benefits, giving the centres in the hands of local groups themselves, building networks at the supra-village level in a so-called People's Organisation, doing away with centrally appointed and paid facilitators and working with volunteers, distributing hundreds of educative folk songs and stories for use in the organisations.

An Indian doctoral student at our department made a qualitative analysis of the 2 to 4-year educational process in 4 villages where APSSS had implanted centres: two which were judged to be "successful" and two "unsuccessful" by their supervisors. (Puli, 1988). This is the start of his thematic chronological analysis of the process in the successful "Pura" village, based on his participant observation: 'It began with the interactions between the facilitator and the community members. The week-long consultations resulted in the establishment of an adult education class. The initial interaction helped to create mutual confidence and a friendly atmosphere between the facilitator and the learners, and among the learners themselves. ...Participants began to learn to read and write and engaged in a discussion. A month-long participation in the class resulted in the setting up of a collective savings fund with the help of the facilitator. A few days later.... the participants initiated an action to acquire government distributed house-sites. They approached the government through the village accountant and got sanctioned 30 house-sites, but they did not accept the offer, since they did not obtain even half the sites they requested. After a brief discussion in the class, they sent the facilitator to the district revenue office to find out about the possibilities for 70 sites. In the district office a sympathetic functionary helped the facilitator by providing the required information and by indicating the necessary steps to take... With this information, they approached an upper caste leader of the village for help. Four months later, they got the requested 70 house-sites. In the same period, they realised the importance of having an organisation of their own. This awareness and their experience in getting house-sites contributed to form an organisation. In the beginning their organisation had no formal structure. With the progress of the program, it took a more definitive shape' (o.c. p. 229- 230).

As the reader will have noticed, this is a "successful case". Even though this does not appear so clearly at first sight, there occurs a combination of two kinds of processes: the teaching-learning process of literacy and numeracy, and the group process of discussion on temporary issues and the planning of actions to undertake. Apparently, the formation of a literacy class goes hand in hand with the setting up of a socio-economic and political organisation. This is exactly what APSSS was looking for. The analysis of all four cases showed, however, that 'soon after the beginning, a shift takes place from literacy-oriented education to issue-and-action-oriented education, which reduces the possibilities of acquisition of literacy skills by the learners'. At the same time, the position of the facilitator was crucial: 'The facilitator's personal integrity, commitment and dedication are most important for the success of the adult education program, because he acts as a model that participants look up to' (o.c., p. 303)

The reorganisation of APSSS, undertaken towards the end of the 80's, took into account some of these evaluative outcomes, and in fact tried to make true the device 'organisation by the poor for the poor'. It apparently met with some success, since in 1991, one counted ca 500 such local organisations with an average of 90 members, grouped in some 100 units or inter-village networks. In a society divided in three layers of castes ("forward", "backward" and "scheduled or lower"), these and other efforts for and with the rural poor are having more than a symbolic meaning. In the recent political history of India, there has already been a first major clash between the powerful parties over giving better social, cultural and political opportunities to the lower, so-called "untouchable" classes. "Awakening education", as we could witness ourselves on stage, is making its small but significant contribution.

Our practical examples, down to the latter one, also make us aware of the limits of the culture of prophetic education and learning. First of all, there is the small borderline between conscientisation/value transmission and indoctrination. Freire himself warned repeatedly against the tendency of old as well as new social movements and leaders to become "oppressors". Related to this is the tendency to see reality through one's normative lenses, and to exchange SEIN and SOLLEN. We are reminded here of a famous verse in Hölderlin, when "the prophet" concludes "that things cannot be, which must not be". Furthermore, the culture of prophetic education tends to impart the myth of leadership-without-power: "charismatic" leaders would, because of their moral integrity, be elevated beyond any power relationships, since they "set free" their followers. Systems theory, which was discussed in the first chapter, comes to quite contrary conclusions when it formulates the following "grammar rules": "people and social groups cannot stay out of the dynamics of influencing one another", and "we should always ask ourselves: Who does What to Whom at what moment?" (Mattheeuws, 1976). Another limitation of the prophetic culture of education is the "integration of reflection and action". We already noticed a comparable integrative tendency in the engineering culture between "work" and "learning". The pre-cited analysis of action-research projects indicates that this integration does by far not succeed as often as its proponents would like. Finally, the culture of prophetic education and learning is sometimes invoked to cure ills which it cannot remedy: when the problem is one of lack of expertise or technical or organisational know-how, an orientation to "new values" or a call for "moral rearmament" will not bring any meaningful solution. We are reminded here of Mao Tsedongs "cultural revolution", where some laudable principles - like that of the solidarity between intellectuals and workers - were applied to revolutionise the organisation of labour and production or to stop scientists from searching for truth and technical progress.

On the other hand, the culture of prophetic education and learning regularly posits a threat to systems and people who try to prevent the blossoming of autonomy, justice and freedom. While discussing a recent military coup and its educational implications in a developing country, we constructed the following 'critical joke':

In a country called Democratura, the new junta decided that it was time to "inform the people about the principles of the revolution and the participation of the people". They launched a campaign, and thus, one information officer went to a village community centre, which had now been renamed as "people's revolution house". A curious crowd of about 80 people had come to listen to him.
He gave a long speech, explaining the principles of the people's revolution. Suddenly, a woman raised her hand, interrupting him: 'Sir, can I ask a question?'
'Certainly, he said, our junta wants our people to ask questions'
'Can we publicly discuss what you are saying?'......
The officer looked grim, and replied: 'Our junta has decided that, for the time being, there will be no more discussion.'
He went on with his speech.
Another hand was raised. 'Sir, why can there be no discussion?' He retorted, angrily: 'This is enough. From now on, no more questions'.
While he went on with his speech, the audience stood up and started leaving the room. 'Why are you leaving, he asked the last person near the door, I have more things to say..' She looked at him, smiled, and said: 'We need not stay any longer. We have understood your message. We are taking it home'...
'We shall meet again' the officer shouted, when the woman had already left the room.

THE CULTURE OF COMMUNICATIVE EDUCATION: TO BE IS TO COMMUNICATE, TO LEARN IS TO DIALOGUE

Disrupture, disjunction, the great turning point, the end of the 'Grands Discours', the end of modernity. These and other expressions abound in the literature and the discussions on culture and education of the early 1990s. Some people tend to see this as a mere fad, or the expression of a cult of "fin de siècle" - and humanity has known such cults before. Let me confess that I too was fairly sceptical about what I called the "doomsday rhetoric" of some so-called post-modernists. But when one starts to look closer into the so-called post-modern movement, one soon finds that we are confronted with far more than a game of words or a fashion show, but with a multiple head-on criticism of cherished concepts, models and practices.

In the world of education - at least in the western part of it - the "anti-modernist movement" has known several tidal waves. I will recall two such waves: the "perspective transformation" of the younger Frankfurt School and what we could call the "French deconstruction movement".

In the previous chapter, we referred to German emancipatory pedagogy, and its main source of nourishment, the Frankfurt School of the "second generation" with authors like Negt, Offe and Habermas. Jürgen Habermas detected three "knowledge-guiding interests", and found the "emancipatory" one to be superior to the "technical" and the "practical" one, since it offered perspectives of liberating people "through power-free dialogue". He found the most illustrative example in Freud's psycho-analytical theory and praxis, because it demonstrates how methodical self-reflection in an open and non-repressive dialogue, can liberate human persons from their suppressed dependencies. He thought to find another good example in the student protest movement of the end of the 1960s.

That movement, however, failed worldwide to reach its "participatory" objectives, and the broader belief in the "revolutionary" force of the workers movement was disconfirmed by the real situation. H. Marcuse, former colleague of Habermas, came to the conclusion that workers had become "associated producers" in the modern market, and that people, generally, 'recognise themselves in their consumption goods, they see their soul reflected in their car, their Hi-FI, their kitchen machines' (Marcuse, 1969). In consequence with his analysis, he spurred on young people to "a great refusal" of the actual system. Habermas, who clearly saw the failure of the

"Frankfurt project", went another way. Leaving his rather vague concept of "dialogue" for what it was, he started to explore new linguistic theories of the speech act, such as those of Austin and Searle, analyzed the process of discursive argumentation, and reconsidered all his former theories of the progress of science, culture and society. (Austin & Searle, 1979). This lead to the publication of a two-volume book under the title *Theorie des kommunikativen Handelns* - Theory of communicative action (Habermas, 1981). The book was published under a blue cover, and this colour was not seen as an indicator of a political switch, but connected to the psychological symbolisation of intellectuality and rational depth. Several readers found it so difficult that they spoke of the "blue monster". Like the French-jewish philosopher E. Levinas, Habermas needs able translators, and has found them e.g. in the Dutch philosopher H. Kunneman (Kunneman, 1983). The Netherlands were definitely the country where the study of and the discussion about Habermas' works received the greatest attention in the 1980s.

I cannot, of course, pretend to synthesise the theory of communicative action in a few pages. On the other hand, one cannot discuss the "communicative culture" of education and learning without taking into account Habermas' central arguments. Therefore, a kind of thematic reconstruction will be attempted here, based also on the analyses of two young colleagues (Masschelein, 1987; De Aguirre, 1989)

Habermas has in fact developed two related theories: one about the basic nature of human existence (the human 'lifeworld') and one about the evolution of society and its institutions (the economical-political 'system'). Let us first concentrate on the theory of the human lifeworld.

The traditional way of thinking about man and human existence is subject-oriented. "Subject philosophy" views man as an I which develops knowledge of and power over the "objective" world of the others and of nature. This position can no longer be held, says the author, since human existence is basically *intersubjective*. The 'We' of culture and society not only exists before the 'I', but is simply constitutive of every individual person: the I can only grow as a person through *communicative action*. This decisive turn of view is well illustrated by South African bishop Tutu's reaction to a reminder of Descartes 'Je pense, donc je suis'. Instead, he said, we should say: 'Because you were all there, I am'. Interaction between humans is as important for society as work and labour, and humans interacting with one another do so from an inherent *normative* point of view. This becomes clear when one analyses the *speech act*. When we truly communicate, we do so on the basis of three "Geltungsansprüche" or validity claims:

- we are referring to 'objective' reality - stating that something 'is as it is'; this is the *propositional* aspect of communication or the claim to *objective truth* (Wahrheit);

- we are referring to a set of values and norms which we commonly share and understand as being right; this is the *illocutionary* aspect of communication or the claim to *exactness or congruity with social norms* (Richtigkeit)

- we want to make it clear that we fully endorse what we say and express what we truly feel, this is the *expressive-aesthetic* aspect of communication or the claim to *authenticity* (Wahrhaftigkeit)

'The speaker thus claims truthfulness for his statements or presuppositions about reality, exactitude for the legitimately ordered actions and their normative context, and authenticity for the expression of subjective experiences' (Habermas, 1981, p. 149 - our transl.)

Communicative action is, briefly stated, a truthful, norm-respecting and authentic exchange of meaning among members of a socio-cultural community. A speech act only succeeds, according to Habermas, 'when the other accepts its inherent offer, i.e. when he says YES or NO to claims which can be criticised' (Habermas, 1981, I, p. 387) Looking back at our 'critical joke' at the end of the previous chapter, we there witness unsuccessful speech acts : the 'information officer' claims to tell the objective truth, to be in congruence with social norms and to believe in what he says. The audience wants to question that, but is rejected. They leave, saying they have understood his lies...

The three inherent claims in fact imply a far broader concept of 'the world' than existed before: human interaction through the speech act includes *objective reality* as well as *social* and *subjective reality* in one and the same action. Communication deals simultaneously with events, with norms and with feelings. Let us note, here, that communicative action does not necessarily presuppose the direct presence of any others: communicative action cannot be reduced to a "group discussion" or an "interview" - even though it will often happen there - but may also take on the form of a written letter, an imaginary meeting or even an "interior monologue". And many so-called group discussions do not meet the criteria enounced above.

The context in which we communicate is that of the *human lifeworld*, which constitutes a 'reservoir' of intersubjectively shared frameworks of interpretation, norms, orientations, needs and identity models which mediate our actions. Hanna Arendt, to whom Habermas is much indebted, uses an eloquent metaphor to denote the nature of the human lifeworld, in calling it a 'Bezugsgewebe' or *relational web*: 'Given the fact that people are not simply thrown into this world, but are born into a world of people already in existence, the relational web of human affairs precedes all single acting and speaking'. (Arendt, 1987, p.174, our transl.)

The term 'reservoir' symbolises two basic aspects of the lifeworld: it is "simply there" as an "unquestioned stock of everyday knowledge", and it is all-encompassing and can never be fully drawn on the scene of conscious dialogue. Whereas the emancipatory pedagogues stated that "one never knows one's own social and personal dependencies", the communicatively oriented ones will state that "one never fully knows and grasps one's own lifeworld". But there is more to say about the lifeworld! Basically, it contains three different structures: *cultural frameworks*, *social institutions* and *personalities*. Culture provides interpretations of reality, the social institutions guarantee solidarity and social coherence, and persons dispose of communicative skills which make them "accountable". Given its threefold structure, the lifeworld fulfils three basic functions: cultural reproduction, social integration and "socialisation", i.e the maintenance and renewal of personal competencies. As one can see, the "lifeworld" is far more than "the inner world of the person", and therefore exceeds our usual "psychological" definition-in-use of this term.

In view of the complex and comprehensive structure of the lifeworld, one could wonder what the basic goals of human existence can or ought to be: knowledge acquisition, or integration or personal competence, or all three? The answer of Habermas is quite simple, but at the same time quite challenging: communicative action is directed at *common agreement* ('Einverständnis'), as the result of a *process of searching for mutual understanding*. This in fact means that there is no final truth, no forever-valid-norm, no completed personality. At the same time, there cannot be any truth separated from ethical norms and personal experience. At this point, communicative action constitutes a rupture with "modern" thinking: 'Our concepts of "action" and of "politics" are similar to that of "education", because they are understood ...on the base of the experiences of "modern" man: the experience to be the source of meaning and the effector of aims ("the creator"). The traditional concept of action used in pedagogy is based in fact on the identification of action with constructing, operating, creating or expressing something' (Masschelein, 1989, p.. 4-5). Such a statement immediately raises a problem: if, as it seems, everything depends on common agreement or 'consensus', can we be confident that the result will be more than a quick and superficial agreement, a "useful compromise"?

The answer to that question lies in the necessary transition from simple communicative action in a self-evident and unquestioned lifeworld to a true *discourse*. Sometimes, critical events force us to make the transition, sometimes we try to purposefully organise it. But as was said above, not every discussion is truly discursive, nor can it be planned on beforehand. Kunneman deduces four conditions from Habermas' writings about the "ideal speech situation", which have to be fulfilled before a discourse can be successful:

1) there should be *communicative symmetry* or *absence of great power differences*, which could prevent some people from expressing their opinions or feelings;

2) participants ought to interact in an *authentic way*, so that no manipulation of other people's feelings takes place;

3) there ought to be an *equal opportunity to participate* for all those involved;

4) all participants should dispose of an equal opportunity to *formulate arguments and counter-arguments*.

Looking at such conditions, one may conclude that we are witnessing the birth of a new utopia, the utopia of communicative equality, one that Mannheim might have classified under his fourth, "socialist-communist" category. Are we dealing with a theoretical and abstract concept, or are we talking about human praxis? A reader of Habermas does not always know at what level the author is speaking. Habermas himself may have given raise to that impression by not differentiating clearly enough between the two levels of analysis: the abstract-normative one of the "ideal speech situation", and the empirical-analytical one of actual human interaction. At the formal-abstract level, he introduces communicative action as the *basic concept characterising all social (inter-)action*: to exist is to act communicatively. At the same time, he speaks of two "orientations" which one encounters in everyday life: a communicative one, oriented towards "*mutual understanding*" and a strategic one, oriented towards "*influencing*" or "*reaching results*". These "types of action" (Handlungstypen) are each other's opposite. The first one aims at reaching a concrete consensus, the second one at obtaining clear results or realising specific intentions. This proves that Habermas is well aware of the difference between "theory" and "practice". However, by using the same term of "communicative action" for two different levels of analysis, he creates a misunderstanding. "Communicative action" is most often used as the *constitutive concept* for all human action at the formal-theoretical level. (De Aguirre, 1989, p. 33).

From the perspective of the theory of communicative action, as Masschelein argues, all education is and cannot be anything else but basically communicative. (Masschelein, 1981, p. 315 f.) Thinking of the two levels of analysis, however, we may ask whether we "see" and "experience" nothing but that in actual practice? Investigating some examples of peace education, De Aguirre finds a pendular movement between "communicative" and "strategic" action in the concrete educative process, even though educators often proclaim to act communicatively. I will come back to this debate in a moment.

A broad concept like that of lifeworld might seem sufficient to cover both the life of the individual and the whole of society: what is there outside of culture, social integration and socialisation? However, to identify the lifeworld with the whole of society would be a mistake in Habermas' view: it would mean one looks at society from the perspective of the "participant" or the "inner side", which is, of course, subjectively coloured. At the same time, we need an "observer's perspective", which reveals there is a "system out there", operating apart from, and sometimes against the lifeworld. We do not only have *cultural reproduction* of knowledge and skills, we also have *material reproduction* of goods, services, etc. As Kunneman says, communicative action alone will not bring bread on the table! Both types of reproduction - those by the lifeworld and by the economic-political system - are linked, although one can detect an initial transfer from the lifeworld to the system. Habermas calls this the process of "rationalisation of the lifeworld": by relegating (the care for) material reproduction to economic and political institutions, the lifeworld frees itself from a burden, and concentrates on its central functions of communicating, caring, organising, teaching, socialising... This brings us close to the "well-fare" state, which has taken over the care of individuals and private institutions for education, health, and social welfare, provided that citizens pay their taxes, and assume their responsibilities.

The relationship between the "system" and the "lifeworld" is presented in the general scheme on the next page (Habermas, 1981, ii, p.473; our transl). In this representation, the lifeworld is divided into two sub-systems, which are the mirrors of two subsystems in society: the *economic subsystem* finds its echo in the *private sphere* of the "individual households", and the *bureaucratic system* refers to the *public sphere or public space* (Öffentlichkeit). The relationship between lifeworld and system has been "mediatised", i.e. the "raw materials" of the lifeworld, like the potential to work, the demands for subsistence, and the tendency to social integration, have been transformed into *production factors*, by forceful use of two means: *money* (F) and *power* (P). For everything the lifeworld "offers" (F' or P'), there is a return by the system: the economic system returns income for labour, and goods and services for consumer demands, whereas the bureaucratic system offers all kinds of organisational services for the citizens' taxes, and takes political decisions in exchange for mass loyalty.

To Habermas, this "exchange relationship" is not simply functional and neutral. What we have witnessed in the past and are still witnessing nowadays is that the *system*, by using its strong "media" of finances and power, has penetrated the lifeworld, and in fact *colonised* it, just as 'colonial lords do with a tribal society'. At the same time, the system has *fragmented* the lifeworld and governed it as separate entities. We might think of the Roman adagio 'Divide et impera'. This combined process of colonisation and fragmentation reduces the possibilities of the lifeworld to fully deploy its communicative function. One example of this is the imposture of criteria like efficiency and, especially, productivity, upon spheres where this runs counter to the basic communicative orientation. One can think of family education, of health care, of social services, of cultural work. Sentences like "the end product of our educational system is a well-trained and well-prepared young citizen, who has realised 70 % of the pre-established end terms" clearly express the "colonisation" tendency by the (economic) system.

Habermas' thesis of the colonisation of the lifeworld by the economic and political system(s) may not sound as deterministic as the classical marxist analyses, yet it does not leave much breathing or moving space for coordinated action on behalf of the lifeworld. The only friction between lifeworld and system, which causes embarrassment to the existing powers, appears exactly in those areas where colonisation hits hardest:
- the "green" problems of eroding the organic foundations of the lifeworld,

- the problems of "unmanageable complexity" as they become visible in the nuclear arms race, the risks of nuclear power plants, the manipulation of genes, the endless expansion of data banks with personal-private information,

- the problems of one-sided "overloading" of the communicative infrastructure by the system (e.g. the bombardment with all kinds of forms and questionnaires).

Table 8: The multiple relationships between lifeworld and economical-political
      system according to Habermas

INSTITUTIONAL ORDERING OF THE L I F E W O R L D	EXCHANGE RELATIONSHIPS	MEDIA-GUIDED SUB-S Y S T E M S
PRIVATE SPHERE	1) P'(Ower medium) -----------> Labour power F(Inancial medium) <----------- Income 2) F <----------- Goods/services P' -----------> Consumer demands	ECONOMIC SYSTEM
PUBLIC SPHERE	1a) F' -------------> T a x e s P <------------- Organisational services P 2a) <----------- Political decisions P' --------------> Mass loyalty	BUREAUCRATIC SYSTEM

It is at these "Nahtstellen" or "seams" between the system and the lifeworld that a new "protest potential" has become active, as we see in the green movement, the peace movement, the new women's movement etc. These "new conflicts", which no longer deal with the (equal) distribution of work and income, but with "the grammar of life forms" provide "learning opportunities" and "learning places" where communicative action can fully express itself and, to a limited degree, influence the system.

Although Habermas is not an educationalist, and seldom mentions educative dimensions or themes, the preceding brief analysis clearly shows that his theoretical synthesis has heavy consequences for the educational debate. One could try to "translate" the basic concepts into new educational theories and models. One could also use the Habermas framework as an evaluative mirror for past and present "grand" theories of education. Our colleague J. Masschelein did both in his already cited study. Its title *'Educative action and communicative action'* immediately reveals the stance of the author: he simply *equates education with communicative action* at a theoretical level, and completely rejects any "goal-rational", "instrumental" or "strategic" concept of education:

'To understand educative action as communicative action means: to propound that educative action does not find its ground in the intentionality .... of the educator. The hard core of all education is a communicative praxis which can mediate meaning and freedom, and which only makes intentionality possible. ... The action of the educator cannot be based on his autonomy, the freedom of the pupil is not the freedom of a self-sufficient and sovereign I.'... 'The foundation of education is participation in a common society' (Masschelein, 1987, p. 348 & 350, our transl.)

Hearing and reading this conclusion, one might say: we have heard this message before! Did not Buber speak about education as an 'I-Thou' dialogue, did not Giesecke speak of democratic participation, did not Freire abolish the teacher-learner dualism, did emancipatory pedagogy not characterise education as liberating interaction on the basis of experience? In his last chapter, Masschelein reviews a number of old and new theories and concepts, where one finds clear statements about reorganising the relationship between educator and educatee in a more "egalitarian" way. Let us illustrate this with the example of two authors: Mollenhauer and Buber.

As was indicated above, Mollenhauer stresses the autonomy of young people as competent interaction partners. 'The realisation of this goal ... is made possible by giving the educandus the opportunity to participate in the interaction... It presupposes an equivalence of the interaction partners. But this kind of equality is .. only semblance because it is 'attributed' to the educandus. Mollenhauer interprets educative action as communicative action with a broken intention... The intention of the educandus can express itself because the educator understands it in a certain way, and gives it a chance. He structures the situation in such a way that the educandus can realise his (i.e. the educator's) 'intentions': the educator acts as if the educandus is already competent' (Masschelein, 1987, p. 284-85)

In clear terms, the author sees emancipatory education, as represented by Mollenhauer, as a huge simulation game: an as-if situation, where educators 'give opportunities' and 'structure contexts' whereby 'interaction partners' can 'freely express' their own experiences and intentions. In other words: emancipatory education is a goal-rational instrument to realise something else, a goal which has been pre-established by the educator, or by a movement, an institute, etc.. In a footnote, the author similarly criticises Freire's conscientisation model, because it is still too much oriented on subjectivity. So much for emancipatory pedagogy.

Admittedly, the most radical and explicit defender of "education-as-dialogue" has been Martin Buber, who has been venerated by some Jewish and other groups as the prophet of communal education. It is one of the authors I have kept going back to for the last 30 years. In his most important work, *Ich und Du* (I and thou), Buber distinguishes two fundamental existential modes in the relationship between the I and the outer world: I-Thou (Ich - Du) and I-It (Ich-Es). (Buber, 1923) The encounter between the I and the You constitutes the basis of the *world-of-interpersonal-relations*. The encounter between the person and the material world allows us to have *objective experiences* of things, objects, qualities, etc. This is *the world-as-experience*, which is always oriented to 'something'. The world of relations, on the contrary, has no such object, it is in fact oriented to 'nothing'. The reason for this is that the Other, who appears to me as a Thou, can never be seen as a mere object: 'The person to whom I say Thou, is no object of experience'. On the contrary, the Thou is marked by immediate presence, and by mutuality.

To Buber, education can only take on the form of an 'I-Thou' relationship, if it is to realise its goals of 'selection from the effecting world' (Auslese der wirksamen Welt) so that the other can become more truly a person. It is the task of the educator to make the best selection, not on the basis of his 'predilections' or his 'strivings' nor by calling upon the 'established order' but by making use of his insight into true values and of his "educator's eye". It is his task to love and to guide in a movement of "Umfassung" or "Encompassment". The educative relationship is one of an all-encompassing dialogue, which respects both 'Gegenüber' or 'opposite partners' and, at the same time, unites them on the ground of a common reality.

Buber's description of the educator's role and task constitutes the starting point for Masschelein's criticism: 'The meaning and the statutory position of the educandus are again related to the experience of the educator' (o.c. p. 292) To corroborate this conclusion, he quotes one of Buber's final statements on education: 'Although the all-important thing is that the educator awakens the I-Thou relationship in the educatee, ... this special educative relationship could not become effective, if the educatee would himself assume the encompassment (Umfassung), i.e. would experience the part of the educator in the common situation.' (Buber, in Masschelein, o.c. ibid.)

As we see, no "grand theory" finds grace before the communicative reflecting mirror held up by Masschelein. This in fact means that our three preceding "cultures of education" do not pass the "communicative test". The reasons seem to be clear: the expert culture cultivates rational autonomy, the engineering culture is steeped in technical or social instrumentality, the prophetic culture holds up predetermined values and norms and wants to conscienticize the other(s).

The previous analysis came as a shock to many educationists in the Dutch-speaking area. The author was accused, i.a. of "rejecting any didactic approach, any planning, any influencing by the educator". De Aguirre makes a more sensitive comment, by pointing out that this analysis was to be situated at the abstract-theoretical level, and not at the empirical one. She herself detected a continuous mix or a pendular movement between communicative and strategic action in the four cases of peace education which she explored. (De Aguirre, 1989, p. 179 f..) Yet, at the same time, she did not dare to draw the full conclusion from her own findings: systematic education can, under certain conditions, support and deepen the learning opportunities which are offered by new social movements. Strategic action can support communicative action!

All in all, Habermas' theory of communicative action does not mean a radical breach with whatever he and his Frankfurt colleagues proposed during the emancipatory wave of the 60s and 70s: if rationality is now founded in communicative action, and the subject is integrated in an intersubjective community, and if the lifeworld situates itself well enough at the friction zones with the system, there is a clear possibility for *ongoing rationalisation of the lifeworld*. In other words: transformative action by groups of citizens remains a clear possibility. (Flecha, 1992) And even though there are traces of the old dualistic reasoning of classical marxism, the "system" is not the "devil", and the "working people" are not the "heroes"; the system is differentiated, and takes on the feature of a janus-faced broker: it takes over a number of tasks and institutionalises them, i.e. does service to the lifeworld, but at the same time it asks the high price of loyalty and acceptance of its criteria of efficiency, power and order. And Masschelein does not discard "good intentions" like interaction, dialogue, participation, or communication either, but states that they are most often perverted by the mostly hidden 'intentions' and 'instrumental actions' of the educators. One might add that his was a theoretical study based on the literature, and not on observation of educative processes which were initiated with the intentions specified above.

One of the criticisms made with regard to Habermas' communicative action theory was that it is still centred on the human subject as the central actor in the lifeworld versus the system, and that the belief in rational progress is still preeminent. This is still a "modern" or a "late modern" theory. (Bernstein, 1985)

Such a criticism cannot be made in front of a number of french authors who set out to "deconstruct" modern man and modern society: J. Derrida, J. Lacan, M. Foucault, R. Girard and J. Lyotard. (Derrida, 1962, 1967; Lacan, 1966; Foucault, 1966; Girard, 1978, Lyotard, 1979).

Derrida was one of the first "anti-modernist" thinkers, who started to exercise a new kind of "archaeology": a search for the origins of man as he appears in texts and in institutions. His conclusion was that words and expressions are fluctuating rather than having a fixed meaning. Later on, he circumscribed the human condition by using a curious French neologism: DIFFÉRANCE (instead of the usual différence). This word is new in writing only, because the ear cannot hear the nuance of *A* versus *e*. Différance means two things: to *differ* in the sense of occupying a different space, and to *defer*, i.e. to be situated at different points in time. One only discovers this différance by *deconstructing* several situations, ideas, institutions, etc. Deconstruction - literally tearing down a building - reveals first of all that there is no progress, as modern man likes to believe, and secondly, that events and situations are unique and cannot be compared. He goes so far as to claim that such concepts as democracy and social justice should not just be de-constructed, but discarded entirely.

From his vantage point of psychiatry and psycho-analysis, J. Lacan wonders where the human 'I' finds its origin. The conclusion of his long and cryptic analysis is that human subjectivity is not an original fact, but the result of a 'mirroring' process with other people, and hence it might well be a fiction. Girard, exploring the "founding" of the world and the appearance of man, states that the human individual is the result of *mimesis* or *imitation*, and endless imitation is the source of continuing vio-lence.
Foucault, like one of his sources of inspiration - Friedrich Nietzsche - was mainly interested in the genealogy of social institutions and social conflicts and the power plays behind them. Modern tradition has claimed to "humanize" power, in creating institutions which were said to be rooted in such principles like justice, rationality and freedom. But if one analyses and deconstructs their real functioning - and the prison is a very eloquent case - one finds that nothing in their functioning reflects any of these principles. Instead, one finds plural and even contradictory definitions of such principles: what is right or just for one, may well be wrong or unjust for another. Hence, the universal modern subject is dead.

Perhaps the most influential, and at the same time a very profound author, who coined the term 'postmodern condition' was J. Lyotard. Digging into the sources of knowledge and life orientation systems, including education, he states that there is no final truth, no universally valid goal, no unity. The "Great Discourses", like that of emancipation, are no longer believed in and even rejected. (Lyotard, 1979, p. 60) Educators should stop viewing people as an "educable third party".

In the second half of the 1980s, Post- Modernism became a "new trend", sometimes adorned with near-mythological attributes. As one philosopher remarks, it now has become a common denominator for a wide range of tendencies, from radical individ-ualism to romantic traditionalism. (De Dijn, 1991). Post-modern authors like the ones mentioned above would refute any attempt at constructing a valid definition, since there are no universally valid concepts, truths or schemes of thought. On the other hand, one cannot deny that there is a definite current of "anti-modernism", firmly rejecting Cartesian rationality and fixed truths and moral principles. To Giddens, post- or better, late modernity is characterised by three propositions:

(1) Nothing can be known with certainty

(2) History is devoid of teleology (there is no "progress")

(3) There is a new social and political agenda. (Giddens, 1990)

The first two have become apparent in our brief analysis of the French deconstructionists. The third needs further explanation. Giddens states that the new agenda is determined by the interplay between four forces: *Surveillance* i.e. control of information and social supervision, *Capitalism* i.e. the accumulation of capital through competitive labour and product markets, *Military power* which controls the means of violence and is linked to the industrialisation of war, and *Industrialism* which tries to transform nature into a "created environment". Looking at each of these forces, one can easily understand why Giddens sees the period of late modernity as one where people are confronted with two basic dilemmas: *security* versus *danger* and *trust* versus *risk*. People live reasonably secure in many parts of the world - in comparison to e.g. 50 years ago - yet they feel constantly threatened by the things that make the daily news. They feel comfortable with the products of modern technology, but are well aware of several risks involved in their production and their use.

For our purposes, one of the main results of the post-modern wave is the *de-centration of the human subject*. The aforementioned authors all ask the question of man's origin, and they all come to the conclusion that modernity created the myth of the autonomous almighty subject, but the consequences of that same modernity have been the destruction of that subject. Analyzing the core of post-modern thought, Bauman concludes that post-modernity is basically characterised by *universal strangerhood*.(Bauman, 1992) If this is the core of post-modernity, then Habermas' theory of communicative action is anything but post-modern. In a certain way, the individual was de-centrated there too, but at the same time, made a member of a lifeworld and a speech community which were engaged in a hopeful perspective of rationalisation via a truthful, legitimate and authentic dialogue. De-centration in Habermas is a positive move towards communal society. In postmodernity, de-centration generally ends in the desert of universal solitude.

At this point, the question arises whether education can have any purpose at all? In an already mentioned article about moral issues in adult education, we have commonly tackled this same question, and stated that 'We refuse to settle ourselves in the "nihilistic paradise of postmodern games of deconstruction". But we also refuse to write off postmodern thinking, because every refutation can be deconstructed.' (Leirman & Anckaert, 1992, p.. 270 f.) But what is the way out of the dilemma? One perspective we firmly believe in is what is called a "humanism of the other man", as it has been developed by E. Levinas since 1970. Let us note first that Levinas' work has been marked most clearly by his jewish tradition and jewish philosophers - among whom Buber and Rosenzweig - on the one hand, and by his personal experience of the German concentration camps in World War II on the other. The opening sentence of his book on *Totality and Infinity* (Levinas, 1970) has both a very practical and a deep theoretical meaning: we should beware of the proclamation of moral principles, since they are invoked to justify war and manslaughter.

Levinas propounds a paradoxical view on man. On the one hand, man is a living protest against every possible totalization or submission to a fixed order: man is "séparation", an irreducible identity. But on the other hand, human subjectivity is the result of and the response to an *asymmetric* relation with the other. In the confrontation of the I with the other, the subject is radically questioned "from on high". To express this, Levinas repeatedly uses the biblical image of 'the widow and the orphan' representing the appeal of the other to be accepted and justly treated by me and not - as totalitarian subjectivity would do - to kill or exert violence. This encounter with the other introduces an *ethical dimension* to human existence. The other then is not simply an "alter ego", one more person resembling me and all the others, but the Other (with a capital O). Thus the individual, who implicitly believes that his mission is to *realise total self-development* is radically questioned and called upon to reorient himself to the good of the Other. This does not mean that my autonomy is destructed, but that it is reoriented: the humanism of the self is transformed into a humanism of the Other. Such a reorientation is made possible by the paradoxical relation between my personal separation and the transcendence of the other. I could of course reject the call, and do violence to the other. History is full of examples of that perversion. But the man who 'kills the other with his sword, only finds a dead body at the end of his weapon - the other has forever escaped'.

From the perspective of postmodernism, we can call Levinas' analysis an example of *deconstruction*. At the end of it, we detect a radically new meaning: the seeming contradiction between subjectivity and objectivity is replaced by a fruitful paradox between the objective call for ethical engagement on the one hand and the autonomous answer of the subject to this appeal on the other. Solidarity with and responsibility for the Other constitute the basis of individual and social life on earth. The other option is totalitarianism and destruction of subjectivity. Postmodernists say that there is no "progress" in history. From the vantage point of Levinas' theory of the humanism of the other man, we can only say that history is a mixed venture of destruction and (ethical) construction. We can even detect a dialectical relationship between the two forms of human and social interaction: violence sometimes leads to the declaration of new human rights and the instalment of institutions like the United Nations. In other words: deconstruction does not universally lead to the conclusion of emptiness, violence and solitude.

From this same vantage point, we can state that Habermas, who undoubtedly links the intersubjective lifeworld to the economic and political system, and offers a far more comprehensive perspective than Levinas, nevertheless maintains a certain kind of dualism: the system colonises and divides the lifeworld, the lifeworld seems to be "the victim of colonisation", but is in and by itself "communicative" and therefore "good". Van der Veen views this as 'a rather pessimistic view of the vitality of the people of good will', because Habermas seems to preach the retreat into the personal lifeworld. (Van Der Veen, 1992, p. 190). But is the lifeworld itself all that good? Cannot culture be oppressive, as the current ethnical conflicts between majorities and minorities, or the dominance of temporary fashions prove? And are there not examples of groups and social organisations that limit the possibilities of free thought and creativity of their members although they do not belong to the economic or bureaucratic power system? And do "personalities" always engage in true communicative action, and do they always have to resort to an argumentative debate to reach a consensus ?

The analysis of two types of reaction to the "crisis of modernity" - the theory of communicative action and postmodern deconstruction - in fact results in one common conclusion with two radically different options: the "death of the autonomous rational subject", which is replaced either by intersubjective communicative action or by universal freedom and strangerhood. Habermas propounds values like objectivity, loyalty and authenticity. Postmodernists state that there are no universally valid truths and moral principles, and they offer powerful examples of deconstruction to prove their point. However, another type of deconstruction, the one made by Levinas, leads to another kind of answer: the so-called autonomous subject is radically questioned by the appeal of the Other to "share his home and do justice", and not to resort to violence. The ultimate commandment, says Levinas, is: "thou shalt not kill". Another paraphrase for this might be: "thou shalt not colonize me". Positively stated, the seeming contradiction between subjectivity and objectivity can only be overcome by an ethical response of "caring for the other", which, at the same time, means "to care for oneself". In educational terms, this brings us close to the position of Buber, but with a light complement: education is a dialogue between I and Thou, in which both sides take care of one another's learning possibilities, in the context of a lifeworld and an economic and political system which offer both security and danger, peace and violence, trust and risk.

The currents of thought that dominated the 1980s exerted a clear influence on the world of (educational) research. After we had witnessed the dominance of an empirical-analytical paradigm in the 1960s and a "regulative" or action-oriented one in the 1970s, the scene was now occupied by another paradigm, the so-called *interpretative* or *hermeneutical* one. It was certainly not as new as some people liked to think, since it had been applied in some areas and fields of research like those of cultural anthropology and oral history since the beginning of this century. In his analysis of models of policy-research, Hutjes similarly speaks of three models: the "distance model", where science is seen as independent and critical, the "service model", where science acts as a supplier of information in order to help shape policy, and the "interaction model", where researchers try to find a good balance between independence and "good communicative commitment" (Hutjes, 1985) In this approach, researchers no longer take the stance of "distant, objective observers" nor of "engaged action-partners" but of *virtual participants to the lifeworld of people*. The effort being undertaken can generally be described as follows: researchers try to enter into the experiential world of other people with "open eyes and attentive ears", using methods and techniques which are of a communicative nature - like participant observation, content analysis of discussions with feedback, open interviews. The basic aim is to help the lifeworld to express its ideas, feelings and action plans in relation to the economic and political system, as a contribution to an ongoing dialogue and a public debate.

It is clear that such an interpretative paradigm shows a preference for so-called qualitative methods. Another of these is the "Delphi method". Delphi, as those acquainted with ancient Greece know, stands for "consultation of the oracle", which, through its priestess, gives answers to questions asked by pilgrim citizens. In its original version, developed in the 1960s, Delphi means the organisation of a series of written discussions among experts about the probability of future events and their consequences. The experts receive written questions in a first round, their answers are analyzed by the researchers, and fed back to the expert panel in the form of a report, together with a second questionnaire, in which some questions are repeated, and new questions asked. Usually, the whole process is terminated after three rounds with a final report. This original method, applied to such issues as "leisure time in the year 2000", "urbanisation of the future", "the organisation of time in post-industrial society" has been called the *prognostic Delphi method*. In the area of adult education, we find a good illustration in the Dutch project of Stroomberg e.a. concerning future orientations of adult education. (Stroomberg e.a., 1987) with ca 110 experts representing different sectors. The study revealed, i.a. that the experts saw two great "currents" of adult education for the future: vocational and qualification-oriented education on the one hand, and general "free" social-cultural education on the other. Only in the area of adult basic education did the two orientations seem to meet.

One of the problems with this type of research is the abstract and futurological nature of the topics being dealt with, and the tendency to use homogeneous groups of experts who only "give their opinion". At the end of the 60s, M. Turoff introduced a participatory variant, called the *policy-developing Delphi*. (Turoff, 1975) He defines it as follows: 'Delphi as it originally was introduced and practised, tended to deal with technical topics and seek a consensus among homogeneous groups of experts. The policy Delphi, on the other hand, seeks to generate the strongest possible opposing views on the potential resolutions of a major policy issue. In the author's view, a policy issue is one for which there are not experts, only informed advocates and referees. The policy-Delphi also rests on the premise that the decision-maker is not interested in having a group generate his decision; but rather, have an informed group present all the options and supporting evidence for his consideration'. W. Faché, who used this variant of the method for several projects in Belgium and the Netherlands, calls it a "participative Delphi". (Faché, 1992, p. 1O8)

Following a congress on future policies for (adult) education in the Flemish community of Belgium, we set up a similar Delphi project in 1990 under the title: *Adult education 1992: towards a supply that covers the needs and a better coordinated policy of lifelong learning in Flanders.*(Leirman e.a., 1992) In this project, two types of issues were put forward: the actual learning needs of adults and the degree of (non)response by adult education organisations, and the (non)coordination of adult education policies in our community. The sample selected consisted of about 300 actors in the field of adult education in Flanders/Belgium. They exerted one or more of the following roles: policy maker, educationist, educational researcher or critical commentator, and were involved in one of the following five sectors: basic adult education, vocational education for 15-21 year olds, vocational/professional adult education for persons above 21, social-cultural work c.q. general or liberal adult education and senior citizens' education.

In terms of contents, our approach was to move from the question "What are, according to you, the major PROBLEMS and CHALLENGES confronting adult persons in the society of the 1990s?" to ensuing questions about GOALS, educational OFFER-INGS and general and specific POLICIES of the authorities, now and in the future. The method used was, as we stated above, that of a policy-developing Delphi i.e. three progressive rounds of written discussions based on questionnaires and reports. After the three rounds, we produced a synthetic report and organised a "Forum-day", where the results, and especially the proposals for practice and policy were discussed with 110 participants. We then drew up a final report, enriched with theoretical reflections on goals, policy and Delphi methodology and a general overview of findings and suggestions. (Leirman, Faché, e.a., 1992)

At the end of this project, we undertook a one-round survey, using questions from the three rounds, in the French-speaking community of Belgium, together with a group of 21 students of the FOPA-institute at our sister university of Louvain-la-Neuve. Together with these students, we also organised a colloquy with some of the respondents in the summer of 1992. (Leirman & Fopa-students, 1992)

Let us look here at a few of the major findings and conclusions of this Flemish Delphi project, comparing them from time to time with what we found in the French community.

In our first Delphi-round, we received 86 answers, fairly equally spread over the different roles and educational sectors. Our first open question of Round 1 resulted in the naming of 271 different problems or issues. Content analysis of the answers lead to the identification of 21 different problem areas, from "Demographic changes" (like immigration and the ageing of the population) and "mobility of persons" to "Environmental pollution", "Complexity of society" " Social inequality ", "threats to Income" (caused i.a. by unemployment) "Difficult access to information" and "Lack of meaning to life".

In Round 2, we fed back this set of problems, and opened with two general questions: "To which degree do adults experience these problems ?" and "To which degree can adult education help solve these problems ?" (on a 7-point scale). We asked the same questions in the French community. The overall results are presented in the following Figure:

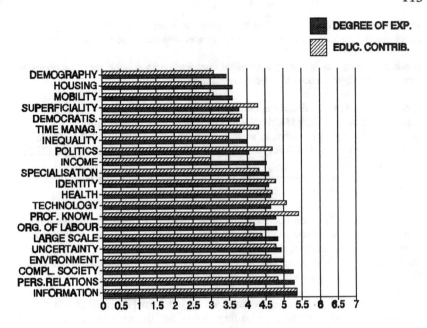

Figure 10: Degree of perceived problem experience and of perceived contribution by adult education (Flemish Delphi project, 1992)

Our Delphi-panel sees five serious problems for adults in our society: the overload c.q. the inaccessibility of INFORMATION, tensions in the field of INTERPER-SONAL RELATIONS within the family and the work sphere, the COMPLEXITY OF SOCIETY, ENVIRONMENTAL POLLUTION, and personal UNCERTAINTY and lack of MEANING TO LIFE. Fairly serious problems are the CONTINUOUS ENLARGEMENT OF NATIONAL TO INTERNATIONAL SCALE, the DEMAND-ING ORGANISATION OF WORK AND LABOUR, the lack of PROFESSIONAL KNOWLEDGE, the difficult access to TECHNOLOGY, the threats to HEALTH, the securing of PERSONAL IDENTITY and continuing SPECIALISATION and threats to PERSONAL AND FAMILY INCOME.

Finally, there are a number of problems receiving a far lesser degree of importance attached: RESTRICTED DEMOCRATISATION, SUPERFICIALITY IN CON-SUMER SOCIETY, MOBILITY, HOUSING AND ACCOMMODATION, and PROBLEMS ARISING FROM CHANGES IN DEMOGRAPHY.

A factor analysis revealed three basic factors in this problem set: personal life problems, problems related to professional life and labour, and problems related to the functioning of society. It was clear to us, that the Flemish panel attached the greatest importance to the first and the second set of problems. Even though we did not find any statistically significant differences between Flemings and Walloons, the french-speaking panel attached a relatively greater importance to societal problems.

The next question was that of a possible contribution to solving these problems by means of (adult) education. Our figure reveals three trends:

1) our panel is fairly optimistic about three problem areas: PROFESSIONAL KNOWLEDGE, INFORMATION and TECHNOLOGY (in that order);
2) a moderate optimism reigns in areas as COMPLEXITY OF SOCIETY, PERSO-NAL RELATIONS, UNCERTAINTY, IDENTITY, ENVIRONMENT, POLITICS and HEALTH;
3) Our panel is moderately pessimistic in problem areas like MOBILITY, DEMO-GRAPHY, INCOME, HOUSING

This differentiation in "educational belief" is fairly well in tune with the actual dominant trend in adult education, where the highest attention is given to professional knowledge and technology, and where the mode of education called training plays a predominant role. The same can be said of the French community, even though technology seems to play a less important role there.

As we already indicated, in our research we moved from PROBLEMS to GOALS. We asked the panel to formulate what they saw as the "five most important goals for adult education" and received 210 goal formulations. We again made a content analysis, and projected it against the framework of adult education goals (both general and specific), developed by K. Martin and A. Todd in a similar research project in the province of Alberta, Canada. We were able to classify the largest part of the answers of the Flemish panel into their nine major Categories - from "COMMUNICATE" and "LEARN HOW TO LEARN" to "EARN A LIVING" and "USE MATHEMATICS", as indicated in our figure below. However, looking at the content of our material, we had to add two categories which we felt were missing from a European point of view: "GIVE MEANING TO LIFE" and "PARTICIPATE IN CULTURE". In Round 2, we again asked our panel to tell us "How important are each of these goals in your eyes?" and "To what degree does the field of adult education effectively work on these goals ?" We present the results in our next figure.

As one can see, all goals are found to be important-to-very important, with six top priorities: COMMUNICATE, LEARN HOW TO LEARN, RELATE TO OTHERS, DEVELOP SELF, GIVING MEANING TO LIFE and FUNCTION AS A CITIZEN. At this point we found a significant difference with the French community. There, the most important goal was FUNCTION AS A CITIZEN, and societal goals were more important there than personal development goals.

Looking at the degree of implementation, one immediately notices that our panel thinks that the degree of attention in actual practice falls far below the degree of importance in most goal areas. Only one important goal appears to find a fair degree of attention: that of COMMUNICATING. This is also the area where panel members

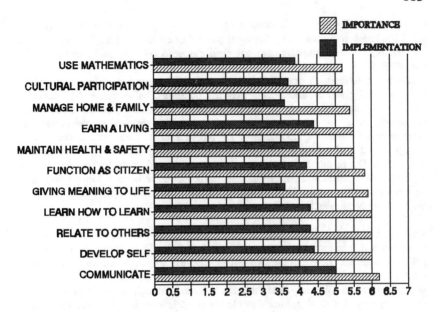

Figure 11: Perceived importance and degree of implementation of adult education goals (Flemish Delphi project, 1992)

signal most innovations in recent practice, especially in the sense of language learning and learning how to work in groups. The area revealing the smallest discrepancy in absolute terms is that of EARNING A LIVING, especially in the sense of professional training. Here too, panel members signal a great amount of innovation.

The biggest discrepancy is found in the area of GIVING MEANING TO LIFE: this very important goal receives rather poor attention, and panel members signal very few innovations in this area. Notice also that the same applies to CULTURAL PARTICIPATION and to MANAGE HOME & FAMILY. When we added the first two items to the original list of nine goal areas, we expected that these would be "strong points" of adult education in our country. Instead of that, our panel signals that there remains much to be done, and this in virtually all areas. Furthermore, there were no significant differences between the five sectors. In Round 3, we therefore asked the question what should be done to narrow the greatest gaps which were signalled? We received a lot of suggestions, and, next to those to be expected (better programmes, more advertising, more support, etc.) there was a fairly large group of panel members who said that in these areas - and also in that of functioning as a citizen - we should incorporate to a far greater extent drama, art and creative expression.

116

Let us note, finally, that the "shortened version" of this project is now being repeated in 14 European countries, using "national panels" of ca 100 people. This will lead to national reports and symposia, and one final european colloquy in Barcelona in the fall of 1995.

Looking at this research example, one detects indeed a number of "communicative" intentions and practices: researchers may ask questions, but establish them together with a "steering committee", do not pre-construct all contents, do not offer hypotheses or theories for being put to the test, and even if they reduce the answers to more or less manageable reports, these are fed back to the "authors". In our Delphi, there was and is also a final colloquy, devoted especially to future issues of practice and policy. The results are convergent in some areas and divergent in others. From there on, practitioners and policy-makers can (could) make better informed decisions. And researchers can start (re)formulating theories about lifelong learning, and thus move to another research paradigm.

Research has, on the whole, not been the area where the culture of communicative education and learning expressed itself most forcefully. That honour goes to several fields of practice. Looking for "known" examples, we might go back to ancient Greece again, and to the "midwife-type of education" of Socrates, as it was escribed in the introduction. We only hear "the master" speak through the voice of his friends and colleagues, but these testimonies clearly point in one direction: knowledge and virtue are developed through authentic interaction. Another example, in the same line, is found in the different forms and practices of "open dialogue" from Augustine's times, over some medieval schools and universities, and to some "lycea" of the Renaissance, as they are described by Ballauff in the work we cited before. (Ballauff, 1985, passim). Coming closer to our days, we may point to the "community school" viz "community college" as thought out and practised by Henry Morris. (Ree, 1971) Even though labels do not always cover what they announce, several other forms of community education - and especially those who stimulate the delicate balance between "the community of people of good will" and the society, as Van der Veen delineates it, and as we could experience it in the KREMAB-project described in the third chapter, are engaged in processes of communicative learning. (Van Der Veen, 1992)

What K. Staessens described earlier on as "the family-type" culture of grammar school corresponds in several ways to the communicative culture of education: the headmaster is "always available for any conversation" as a father-figure, he is "part of the team", that team works as a "village fanfare", and the school atmosphere is one of care and friendly cosiness. On the other hand, one problem here may be that the basic goals and the demands by the outer world to innovate are seldom commonly discussed. In other words, authenticity is a high priority, adaptation to social norms is a far less urgent matter.

A more convincing example in the realm of school education for young children seems to me the so-called "experience-oriented pre-school education", as it was developed i.a. by F. Laevers, and recently consecrated in an international conference. One of the basic concepts here is "betrokkenheid" or "involvement" between teacher and children and among the children themselves. (Laevers, 1992) Another area of communicative education is, of course, that of group work, and especially those types where the focus of attention is not mainly or exclusively to the group task, but to interpersonal relationships, group climate and personal well-being. The same can be said of socio-cultural free associations and of the so-called "study circles" in Scandinavian countries.

Communicative education and learning are not restricted, however, to the so-called "soft" domains of schools, community centres, reading clubs, group work training centres. The "fourth path to innovation" described by Bouwen e.a under the name *the learning-confrontational model* bears great similarity to what is analyzed here. (Bouwen e.a., 1991, p. 46 f, slightly rev. in Bouwen, 1992.) Let us look at one concrete example:

MATERIALS is a Belgian branch of an American multinational which produces insulation materials. During the 60s and 70s, they realised a growth rate of ca 20 %, but were confronted, in the 80s, with a crisis. Leadership was aware that they had to become more flexible and more customer-oriented. Until then, the plant had developed a 'culture of informality, individual responsibility and creativity'. But that culture came now under pressure.

Two different and at first separate reactions arose. The mother organisation wanted to install full-automatic systems for handling materials and products in all plants, which would shorten delivery times. On the other hand, there was a call for an Integral Quality Control project. The local management decided to join these two efforts. The total process lasted four years. We will only mention a few key persons and key moments. After a three-day seminar, they held weekly project group meetings and decided upon the following general objective: "To have an efficient organisation (policies, people, tools) in terms of customer service (delivery, quality), cost control (working capital, overhead) and integration of new products and processes" Looking at this formulation, we seem to be located at the "economic system side" of Habermas' scheme, rather far away from the "lifeworld" of the people involved. But then, they also decided on a set of five working principles:
- everyone can speak freely and receives the time required;
- no point is excluded from the discussion;
- we take our time, and don't let ourselves be manipulated by external pressure;
- progress is made according to the principle of consensus;
- once we have reached this consensus, we stay by it.

Gradually, the group developed the idea of constructing a matrix of tasks to be fulfilled (What?), with the corresponding functions (Who?) Specification of tasks was not too difficult, but who would fulfil them? There was much tension about this question in the group. At one moment, the product manager, leader of the group, invited members to volunteer. He recalls: 'Mr X. stood up and proposed himself openly as a candidate. I could not agree with that and said so. I proposed to him to run another production line. The others hesitated... Then I made public my proposal and wrote some names on the organisation chart. There was a general relief in the group at that moment. I left for a while then. Entering again, the first one who replied was X and he said: "I go for it". Still more names were filled in during that meeting. In fact, a lot of further thinking had to be done. I talked to a lot of people before a complete proposal could emerge.'

The group did not only hold regular meetings at the workplace. On a few occasions, they took a "time-out" to look back at what they had done, and listened to the observations of a member from the personnel section who took that role.

As a result, five new product groups were formed, based on the concept of the "focused factory", i.e. a work organisation which is regrouped around a small number of major tasks, and integrates all different kinds of personnel.

Bouwen concludes his narrative as follows: 'The most important quality of this innovative path is the two-sidedness of the communication process. The characteristics of Argyris' and Schön's (1978) model II organisational learning apply: using concrete, illustrated, and testable statements that are open to any possible reaction from the partner in the dialogue. There is co-ownership of the interaction task and shared influence on the outcomes. The basis for making decisions is consensual validation. (Schein, 1969) This does not mean an overall compromise, but an agreement supported by all parties involved after each of them had the full opportunity to express their concerns, got the acknowledgement of being understood, and joined in the construction of the best available solution' (Bouwen e.a., 1991, p. 48).

On a broader scale, this example fits in fairly well within the concept of the "learning organisation", as it was described in our second chapter. And amazingly perhaps, it is also congruent with the "Kaizen philosophy" proclaimed by Imai in Japan. (Imai, 1986)

Looking at this example and this conclusion from the viewpoint of "true communicative action" as Masschelein did when judging prior attempts at participatory, dialogical education, I am virtually certain that this too would be evaluated as "goal-oriented" and "instrumental" action, under the "pretext" of being communicative.

This brings us to the critical problem of delineating the basic dimensions of the culture of communicative education and learning. If we put ourselves at an abstract-analytical level, then we should refrain from trying to describe a "culture", because that is not only theoretical, but at the same time, very pragmatic and visible. Post-modernists, moreover, may state that the abstract concept of communicative action and its inherent values does not stand the test of de-construction - e.g. due to the fact that it receives many different interpretations and that various and very different practices want to claim it. Instead of saying "there is no room for such an idealistic concept", we here take a more empirical stand. The culture of communicative education and learning contains, like the other cultures described before, a framework for interpretation of reality as well as a behavioral code and a pragmatic identity. Of course, the culture of communicative education and learning is bearer of a view on man and society. The human person is seen as *homo dialogalis*, i.e. not only man-of-dialogue, but man constituted by dialogue and communicative action. Society is seen as a conjunction of two types of community, as Van der Veen pointed out: the *cultural community* of "people of good will", accepting the temporary and fragile balance between individual rights and solidarity, and the *community of the personal lifeworld*. The main goal within this perspective is to further develop and strengthen the capacities of *communicative acting*, which means both dialoguing about and within the lifeworld and asserting its expressive interests towards the outer world. In this sense, the mission of education is to assist (groups of) people in becoming authentic and objectively listening actors, and to stimulate consensus-building against all forms of colonisation and fragmentation. Levinas would term this the resistance against personal and societal totalitarianism. In the last example given, this was very well expressed in the criteria set up for the in-company-work group: free expression of ideas and feelings, take time, resistance to outside pressure, consensual decision-making.

The learning concept which is central to this culture is that of what we called *open experiential learning*, i.e. openness to the expression of one's own, and of other people's experiences and their true meanings. In speech act terms, this is the (continuous) learning of *propositional speech*, i.e. making objective statements about one's lifeworld, *illocution*, i.e.. of realising common understanding and *perlocution*, i.e. expressing oneself authentically both in thinking and feeling. The preferential educational strategy can be called *dialogical-growth oriented*, since it stresses the continuous process of communicative exchange between all actors involved, and is interested in the further development and/or renewal of the personal and the socio-cultural lifeworld.

The educator here takes the position of *communicator* and *facilitator*: s/he tries to combine the communicative strategy of truthful and authentic expression with the strategic interventions of the facilitator who will stimulate and encourage participants to "speak and listen". Participants may also take these same positions, but one could use analogous terms: they are approached as *experts of their own lifeworld* and *partners* in communication.

The strengths of the culture of communicative education and learning have already become apparent through our analysis and the examples given: it strengthens the individual, social and cultural lifeworld; it is based in experience; subjectivism as well as totalitarianism are resisted, and it keeps its distance from outside pressures; decisions are consensual.

But it has its weak points too: it needs and takes time - far more than is often "officially" allowed, it is exposed to the colonisation and fragmentation of all kinds of systems and institutions, and it is often strategically weak or naive in its expectance

120

to "change systems without using their means of finance and power". Finally, as both Van der Veen and Jansen e.a. indicate, it may yield to the temptation of "aestheticism", i.e. of cultivating the expression of feelings and personal choices and 'failing to introduce the participants to the rich tradition of analyses and arguments to the normative problems at stake' (Van Der Veen, 1992, p. 198) or to 'theoretically informed views and visions of society' (Jansen, 1992, p. 101). From this vantage point, communicative education is not "the educative culture par excellence", but one culture next to others.

CONCLUSION:

A CLOVER-LEAF
OF FOUR CULTURES ?

The retrospective exploration of four cultures of education and learning has come to an end. How shall we conclude now ? A colleague to whom I spoke about the concept of the book, gave me the following advice: 'after you have analyzed your concepts, given your illustrations and produced your schemes, you better look at this mosaic, and wipe it all out. Your final statement should be: these were possibilities, there is no conclusion, we can be sure of nothing.' This looks quite post-modern indeed: after de-construction, there are no constructs any more. Or is a statement like the preceding one simply an expression of a fifth culture of education: that of laissez-faire, in the sense of "let everybody compose his own cocktail"?

We face the undeniable fact of plurality of educative cultures, paradigms, learning concepts and strategies. Nearly all of them claim an exclusive birthright: they are better founded and more apt to solve the problems of our time than any other. This creates quite some confusion, and one may feel tempted to engage in a comparison, lead by the expectation of finding the underlying common denominator, the universal cornerstone. This would follow the Gaia-hypothesis spelled out in the introduction: reality is one, and so are education and learning.

Gaia-paidea, or the mother-image of education as one great family, has always been attractive to educators who believed in global and integrative development of "the community of people of good will", from Socrates to Buber, from Erasmus to Montaigne, from Gandhi to Freire. But given the "lessons of de-construction", we may need to look at that hypothesis again.

One of the ways to do so is to look into one's own educational and learning biography, a move which has become fairly popular these days. Anniversaries of schools, universities and other centres of learning are one occasion to engage into this type of educative archaeology. The director of the "S. Aloysius-college" where I went to

124

school in the 40's and the 50's thus invited me to the celebration of its 125th anniversary in 1988. He wanted me to talk about "education in our modern times". The address was re-titled "To Educate in crisis times: an impossible task?". It contained two parts: a narrative reconstruction of everyday school life in those difficult war and post-war days, and a theoretical part about "the four-clover-leaf of education". The thesis of this latter part was that true education had to look like a clover-leaf of four dimensions: acquisition of basic knowledge and key skills, development of independent critical personalities, development of solidarity, and learning how to care for the others and for nature. A playdoyer was held in favour of a balanced attention to all four components, a task which could not be fulfilled by the school alone, but by a joint effort of all educational milieus, including the family and youth work. Concluding, I stated that a clover-leaf of four was an extremely rare plant, but that at some places and moments in time, we as a class group, thanks also to the engagement of some of our teachers, had the opportunity to detect and enjoy it. (Leirman, 1989)

At the ensuing official banquet, we sat together with a group of former schoolmates who had not seen each other for about thirty years. They did not talk about the clover-leaf theory, but came with their own school stories. One of them said: "what I've learned here was to live in a group and do something together". Another stated: "Here I've laid the basis for my interest in classical culture and in languages". "Not only that, said a third, but also the basic christian values. Remember that our common study room carried the slogan: Ora et labora, pray and work!" These positive statements were followed by remarks about some missing "blanks" like "we did not have enough time for recreation", "the regime was severe" or "I lost a year because of the teacher". I was simply amazed by the variance in basic learning experiences, but, at the same time, by the "old boys group atmosphere". Part of the latter was of course coloured by a nostalgia for "the good old days". Nevertheless, the question remains: were we talking about different schools, or was there just one school? It was clear that my own image of past school education was a mixed one, and that it did only partially coincide with that of others.

At the level of concepts and theories of education, we face the same question: difference, similarity, unity? There may be no country where the debate - or better - the struggle between different schools of thought has been so strongly exercised as (western) Germany. One needs only to point at the "Methodenstreit" or the war-of-methods raging in the field of sociology in the early '70s. At one point, the publication of an empirical survey revealing the significant social or educational retardation of lower social groups was seen as an act of discrimination and exploitation of the working class. Quantitative methods were linked to "confirming the social status quo" and qualitative methods to "emancipation of the underprivileged". One scholar who has witnessed the whole post-war educational debate in Germany is Franz Pöggeler, who became my earliest guide into the theories of "andragogy" or adult education. Although he generally maintained a "hermeneutic" position like his master W. Flitner, he continuously tried to have a good communicative relationship with representatives of the other currents, and hence adapted and broadened his own perspective. This became very clear when he published a book on *New theories of adult education*, together with B. Wolterhoff back in 1981. (Pöggeler & Wolterhoff, 1981). In the introduction the authors review the scene as follows:

'Given the fact that adult education research does not exist in isolation, but within the context of work in the social and the other educational sciences, the different perspectives of these sciences are also reflected here. New methods unearth new aspects of the complex phenomenon called continuing education. Theories and methods like systems theory, communication theory, ... or neo-marxist theories seem to be totally unrelated, but later on, one finds ... parallels and similarities, even to the point of sometimes reaching the same results.

Even though we as editors had thought of arranging a planning meeting with the 15 authors of the present book, these authors have not convened to plan their contributions on beforehand. A clear profile of differences and oppositions is to be preferred over a prefabricated "harmonisation". The fact that we find a plurality of theoretical approaches is not a sign of fragmentation or disunity of the science, but on the contrary a proof of richness and vitality' (o.c., p.8)

One cannot deny that there is a certain ambivalence about the previous statement: theories and methodologies, which seem to be radically different, bear more resemblance than one would think, yet there exists a clear plurality which ought to be expressed and accepted...

Addressing himself to the "new self-consciousness of educational science", P. Smeyers looks into the same problem of the so-called "paradigm-war" in the area of theories on teaching and learning in the school context. Whereas some people suggest that we have now reached a period of peaceful coexistence or even harmony, recent analyses show the contrary to be true. (Smeyers, 1992). An American educational methodologist who was cited earlier, N.L. Gage, describes the 'Paradigm Wars and their aftermath' in a recent article (Gage, 1989). He discerns three war-making paradigms: the positivist, the interpretative and the critical-theoretical. The *positivist* one views education, as we know, as a linear process of influencing and steering observable behaviour. It can be criticised because of its disregard of intentions, of the complex web of interacting variables at play, and of its presupposition that we live in a world as stable as that of nature. The *interpretative position* sees man as meaning-maker and creator of his/her own reality. Here, one can ask whether such an optimistic view of things can be maintained. The *critical position*, finally, rejects the determinism of the social context, and states that people can change social structures. That position too has been severely criticised, i.a. by postmodern authors. To a certain degree, three of our educational cultures enter the scene here: the engineering, the communicative and the prophet culture. Gage holds a playdoyer to "retain the best elements of the three", i.e. to try to integrate them from their strongest points onwards.

126

Could it be then that the difference between these three paradigms, which is sometimes reduced to two, namely a "positivist" and a "naturalist" one, does only exist at the level of the *methods* being used, and not at the deeper level of concepts and axioms? Popularly stated: there are different methods of making wine, and accordingly, one gets various kinds of wine, not only different in colour, but different in texture and taste as well. But after all, the result is always wine! Smeyers convincingly argues that it is not the difference between "quantitative" and "qualitative" methods" that is crucial in explaining the differences between paradigms: we have now reached the point where both types of methods are being used in all of the paradigms.

The so-called positivist approach is interested in "the things as they are", which, given the nature of human knowledge according to Wittgenstein, always means "the things as they are to us, with our interests and values". It retains its meaningfulness, since scientific work aims at understanding reality, trying to detect interdependencies and making predictions about it. But this approach can never fully explain "what people do according to their own experiences and interpretations". Here, the accent is on the "things as we see them according to what is important to us". Educational science, according to Smeyers, is like all sciences in that it tries to do three things in combination: *explain, predict and change*. It has its own identity, not because of any "typical" methodology or methods, but because of its content: the ideas about and the practices of education, training and guidance. At the same time, the different paradigms retain their importance, but he seems to indicate that it is a relative one. At least, he does not reject "positivism" as being non-scientific.

Could this be our own conclusion too, in relation to the four cultures of education and learning described in the previous chapters? In order to answer that question, I want to go back to the basic dimensions of each of the four cultures, and put them side by side. This construct may help us to see whether there are "connections", and what these are. On the next page, a comparative table is presented, with the following horizontal dimensions: the typical *view of man and of society* inherent to that culture, the main *objective* in terms of basic effects to be realised and the typical *"mission"* of education under that culture, the central *learning concept*, i.e. the way learning is defined in process and product terms, the preferred *strategy* and an example of one *process function theory*, the *position of the educator(s)* in their relationship to learners and, correspondingly, the *learner's position*, and finally, the main *strengths and weaknesses* of each of culture. Let us first conduct a vertical analysis of the expert culture in all its dimensions, and then compare it with the other three.

In the preceding chapters, each of the cultures of education and learning have been described and analyzed mainly from a theoretical and normative point of view, stressing, at the same time, the viewpoint of the educator(s). In view of the fact that cultures contain more than norms, action codes and identity profiles, but are at the same time living realities of people-in-action, we could now try to approach this
Table 9: Comparative table of the four cultures of education and learning

CULTURES -> DIMENSIONS ↓	EXPERT CULTURE	ENGINEERING CULTURE	PROPHETIC CULTURE	COMMUNICATOR CULTURE
VIEW ON MAN	HOMO SAPIENS	HOMO FABER	HOMO VIATOR	HOMO DIALOGALIS
VIEW ON SOCIETY	ENLIGHTENED SOCIETY	PROFESSIONALI-SED SOCIETY	MORAL COMMUNITY	COMMUNICATIVE LIFEWORLD
MAIN OBJECTIVE	RATIONALISATION	ACTION PROFICIENCY	RAISING MORAL CONSCIOUSNESS	STIMULATE COMMUNICATIVITY
MISSION	TRAIN CRITICAL CITIZENS FOR AN ENLIGHTENED SOCIETY	TRAIN SKILFUL ACTORS FOR AN EFFICIENT SOCIAL SYSTEM	EDUCATE VALUE-CONSCIOUS CITIZENS FOR FREE & JUST SOCIETY	DEVELOP COMMU-NITY OF ACTORS IN DIALOGUE
LEARNING CONCEPT	COGNITIVE INFORMATION PROCESSING (comparative, goal-directed, network, context)	TRANSFORMATION OF ACTION STRUCTURES (learning-by-doing)	LEARNING TO MORAL MODEL (value transmission, clarification)	OPEN EXPERIENTIAL LEARNING (empathy, illocution, perlocution)
STRATEGY/ PROCESS FUNCTIONS (exemplary)	RATIONAL-EMPIRICAL. 1. KNOWLEDGE SEARCH/ PACKAGING 2. PERSUASION 3. TRIAL/DECISION 4. EXPANSION OF KNOWLEDGE BASE	SOCIAL-TECHNOLOGICAL 1. DIAGNOSIS OF DEFICIENCIES 2. ACTION PLAN 3. TRAINING 4. EXPERIMENT 5. IMPLEMENTATION	NORMATIVE - TRANSFORMATIVE 1. CONCIENTISATION 2. SELF-CONFRONTA-TION 3. MOBILISATION 4. CONSOLIDATION	DIALOGICAL-GROWTH-ORIENTED 1. EXPLORATION OF LIFEWORLD 2. NEEDS EXPRESSION 3. CONSENSUAL ACTION
POSITION OF EDUCATOR	EXPERT / INFORMANT	PLANNER/ PROCESS-MANAGER	CONCIENTISATOR/ MORAL EXAMPLE	COMMUNICATOR/ FACILITATOR
POSITION OF LEARNERS	INFO PROCESSOR/ PROBLEM SOLVER	DECIDER/ "DOER"	MEANING MAKER/ MORAL ACTIVIST	EXPERIENTIAL EXPERT/ PARTNER
STRENGTHS	ANAL. RATIONALI-TY/PROBLEM - SOLVING	PLANNING/ TECHNICAL CREATIVITY	VALUE ORIENTATI-ON /PERSPECTIVE TRANSFORMATION	ORIENTATION TO LIFE EXPERIENCE & COMMUNITY-BUILDING
WEAKNESSES	LOGOCENTRISM: INSENSITIVITY TO VALUES/EMOTIONS	TECHNOCENTRISM: TENDENCY TO ACTIONISM	MORALISATION/ PRAGMATIC SENSE?	DISREGARD OF GLOBALISATION

128

table first of all from a learner's point of view, whether it be individuals, groups or, indeed, organisations.

Entering the *expert culture* of education and learning, people are invited to act as seekers of knowledge and wisdom, to overcome their ignorance and to build a well-informed and critical society. As was stated before, this is the culture of *homo sapiens* or rational man and of a society which has acquired the "light of critical knowledge" to become *enlightened. Rational in-formation* in its different aspects and depths is what learners are looking for: knowledge of facts, explanations, comparisons, frameworks, underlying principles, recognition of structures, putting "things in their actual and historical context", seeing the world in a reflexive mirror... Their hope is that an increase in knowledge will provide them with new powers to master the problems encountered in life.

Ascending the "mountain of knowledge" requires a certain type of learning. Formerly, one saw this as a response to stimuli given by a teacher or a source of information. Nowadays, this rather mechanistic concept has been replaced by a richer and more active one: learners are active processors of information, they "re-order their heads" by taking several steps. An adequate image for this process may be that of an *open and dynamic library*. Learning individuals and learning organisations posses a vast "stock of knowledge". They will not acquire new information without looking at what they already possess.
Yet they may not be fully aware of that, or may not have "systematised it into a useful catalogue". As was shown in our first chapter, children or adults learning basic mathematics or basic literacy do possess quite some knowledge of e.g. addition or of word-construction, but may need time and some help to detect and use the principles behind that. However, "new information" is always "information about something", and the cognitive way of learning is directed at specific goals or contents: the library will not just let all sorts of new materials enter, because that would mean disorder and inaccessibility of the different sections, rubrics, titles and specific contents. Let us note also, that libraries often have different levels or floors, and that access to the cellar or the archives is not easy anyhow! Learning in the expert culture is like enriching one's library, looking for new themes and new contents, and putting the new "material" into the adequate place. The temporary end result is an expanded network of knowledge, and also a "library" which is better adapted to the outside world, i.e. has become better integrated in its physical and social context.

Entering the expert culture of education and learning means more than getting to know concepts of humankind and the ways it may learn. It has its pragmatic side, in that it proposes strategies as global intervention plans for stimulation of the learning process, situated within a certain vision on education. The "typical" strategy of expert education is called *rational-empirical:* it contains a global map for the search of knowledge in continuous confrontation with empirical reality. Several strategies were presented in our first chapter: that of traditional didactics, that of Research-Development-Diffusion and that of Innovation-Decision according to Rogers e.a. For practical purposes, we have tried to integrate these into an overall strategy containing four process functions or teacher/learner operations, looking first at steps taken by learners, accompanied by actions of the educator(s). This is not exactly a "phase theory", because the time sequence may not follow the numeric order of functions, and some functions may, as we have seen, be skipped or reduced to a minimum. The four basic operations are:

(1) the *search for information and valid knowledge* on the side of both learners and educators, and its *packaging* into a rationally structured set of action steps, materials and learning devices;

(2) *persuasion*, i.e. motivation and demonstration of its usefulness by educators and "making up one's mind" by the learners in the form of comparison and mental evaluation;

(3) *trial/decision*, i.e. a mental and, if possible, also a practical try-out of the new information, e.g. in the form of exercises, and a decision as to whether and how the new information can be added to the cognitive action library;

(4) *expansion of the knowledge base/integration*, i.e. building the new information into the existing knowledge base, which may involve a reorganisation and a repositioning towards the physical and social environment.

Let us remind ourselves of the fact that research has shown that a successful completion of this cognitive learning process also depends on a whole range of "antecedent" and "process variables", such as personality characteristics, the existing norms and values, the degree of complexity of the new information, the availability of communication partners and channels, etc.

The *position* taken by the educator(s) here is that of purveyor of expert knowledge and of informant. Knowledge is also the power base from which the educator(s) can influence the learners: they invoke the "authority of knowledge" as it is represented by science, by books and by their own training, in order to "see that the things to be learned are learned indeed". Correspondingly, the position of learners is that of processors of the new information and of problem-solvers: they are the ones who have to "go the whole way" and have to "solve the problems by using their rational powers".

In the first chapter, the strengths and the limitations of the expert culture were indicated. The table reduces this to the basics: the opportunity given to further develop and apply analytical rationality and the further development of problem-solving both in its strategic and its content dimensions are clear strong points, but, as several of our examples proved, the expert culture has a tendency to overlook the real importance of values and of feelings, and their impact on cognitive learning. In its own terms, this is the tendency to "logocentrism", i.e. to view the world as a rational construct.

A first look at the presentation of the three other cultures, can only lead to the conclusion that they are markedly different from the expert culture as well as from their other "neighbours".

This is true, first of all, for the *view on man and the world* inherent to each, and for the main *objective* being pursued: the *homo faber* is not in the first place a thinker but an "architect" of a technically skilful society, the *homo viator* or "pilgrim man" is in search of values rather than rationality or technical skills and wants to create a moral society, and *dialogical man* opposes the subjectivity inherent to each of the three preceding ones, and views existence as communal dialogue between the human lifeworld of culture and personality on the one hand and the social-economical system on the other.

A similar difference comes to light when we look at the main *objectives* and, especially, at the *mission of education and learning*: the engineering culture wants to see a society of skilful actors and efficient social systems, the prophetic culture dreams of a morally conscious, free and just society, and the communicator culture sees the building of an authentically and truthfully dialoguing lifeworld as its inherent mission.

Looking at the core *learning concepts*, the distance between the cultures seems to become even greater. For the expert culture, we used the image of an "active and open library". For the engineering culture, one might use the metaphor of the "skills workshop", where learners acquire their skills by doing, and thus transform their action structures. The historic example of medieval apprenticeship, and the actual one of workplace learning illustrate the basic elements of this type of learning: looking at the example, following the instructions, imitating and experimenting with hands and feet. Within the prophetic culture, we could use the image of the "temple" or "the church", where learners are exhorted to take over the moral model presented to them or by them. This means developing a sensitivity for values and norms, confronting oneself with the ethical model(s) being presented, and interiorising the new norms and values and transforming one's action perspective. In the communicator-culture, the metaphor of the "agora" or the "forum" aptly translates open experiential learning: learners are gathered in a community where they exchange experiences and develop mutual empathy, confront their desired lifeworld with the actual situation, and try to reach a common understanding and an action consensus.

In the area of *strategies* and *process functions*, there seems to be, on the contrary, some *convergence*, at least between the expert and the engineering cultures on the one hand, and the prophetic and communicative cultures on the other. The first two in fact bear a fairly rational character, in working from a type of diagnostic analysis or search down to adoption or implementation, and in stressing the importance of the human subject as an actor of change. A comparison of the prophetic and communicative cultures equally leaves us with the impression of some similarity: both are of the "conversion" type, either as a result of the confrontation between OUGHT and IS, or of a confrontation between lifeworld experiences and the colonisation and fragmentation by the system or within parts of the lifeworld itself.

The same type of similarity appears when we look at the *positioning of educators and learners*. There is not too great a distance between being an expert and an informant, transmitting knowledge to the learners, and being a planner and a process-manager, trying to induce structural changes: both positions are "professional", rational and "transmissive" in nature. Within the prophetic and the communicator culture, the positioning of educators bears *ethical overtones*. This is clearly the case for the "concientisator/moral model" position, and only seemingly less so in the "communicator/facilitator" position. Here too, the educator "gives the good example" and sees to it that "the conditions of a true dialogue" are met!

Similarly, learners who act either as processors of information and problem-solvers or as deciders and doers are close neighbours, since the focus is on obtaining concrete results through personal action. The learner's position in the prophetic culture seems to be clearly different from that of the communicative culture: a "moral activist" wants to "make the others look like his moral model", whereas a "partner in a dialogue" has no such intentions. But as Buber and Levinas told us, and as the examples of the Delphi study and the Materials Case revealed, such a dialogue has binding effects on all participants nonetheless. The difference may reside in the rather individual and pre-structured character of prophetic education versus the consensual and communal character of communicative action.

The comparison of *strengths and weaknesses* leads to yet another conclusion than those of "radical difference" or "partial similarity": the strengths of one culture reappear, in some cases, as the weaknesses of another and vice versa! Thus the expert and engineering cultures excel in rationality and planned strategic action, aspects which are minimised in the "value-stressing" prophetic and the "dialoguing and open-ended" communicative cultures. And the first three cultures accentuate subjective responsibility and action, whereas the last one replaces such an "I"-orientation by the WE of the dialogue.

Thus far, the comparison leads to a fourfold conclusion:

- looking at the underlying world views, the professed objectives and mission statements, and the basic learning concepts, the four cultures clearly stand apart as unique and independent;

- comparing the strategies, process functions and the positioning of educators and learners, we come to a partial regrouping: the expert and engineering cultures constitute a strategic pair of rational change cultures, whereas the prophetic and the communicative cultures constitute a less strategic pair of ethical conversion cultures, either by "preaching" or by "dialoguing";

- an analysis of strengths and weaknesses leads to the conclusion of a possible complementarity of the "positivist" expert and engineering cultures on the one hand, and the "naturalist" prophetic and communicative cultures on the other;

- after all, one basic difference seems to remain: the first three cultures are imbued with a belief in the human subject as a problem-solver, a creator of structural change or a moral reformer, whereas the fourth one rejects subjectivity and professes the existential priority of the intersubjective community.

The question of "difference" versus the possible "interconnection" c.q. an eventual full "convergence" of the four cultures of education and learning receives a different answer at the *normative*, the *strategic* and the *empirical-functional* levels: at the normative level they are clearly different, at the strategic level they can be regrouped in a positivist-pragmatic and an naturalist-ethical perspective, whereas the empirical effectuation level reveals a mutual complementarity of strengths and weaknesses.

The previous comparison is situated at a rather abstract and theoretical level. Maybe going back to some of our practical examples might lead to still other conclusions or, as my colleague expected, wipe out the whole construct. It would take too much time and space to review all of them here - even though I did the exercise personally. Instead, I propose to look at one case, and to add some remarks regarding some of the other examples.

In the fourth chapter, the MATERIALS case was presented as an example of the communicative culture. Let us look back now at some of its decisive episodes:

1) At the start of the 4-year innovation project, a "project group" was formed, which drew up the following statement of goals:

"To have an efficient organisation (policies, people, tools) in terms of customer service (delivery, quality), cost control (working capital, overhead) and integration of new products and processes".

It is very clear that both the language and the contents of this "mission statement" belong to the *engineering culture*, stressing efficiency, action control and a visible change of structure as an end result.

2) However, the work group establishes a set of "working principles" stressing free expression of ideas and feelings, taking time, resisting outside pressures, and consensual decision-making.

These principles all belong to the *communicative culture*! And apparently, the work group respected these all through its four-year effort, as the final evaluation shows.

3) The group commonly constructs a "matrix of tasks and functions" for the future new organisation of the plant: this is a very rational-analytical exercise, which moves the group into the *expert culture*.

4) The group then starts to discuss the "filling in of names for each specific function", and that, understandably, creates high tension. Only one participant ("x") speaks out, and applies for one of the new functions. The others keep silent. Thus, the rule of "free expression of ideas and feelings" is not respected. At this point, the group is unable to stay within its self-selected communicative framework.

5) The group leader then takes the initiative, states that X is not the best candidate for that specific function, and proposes concrete names to functions. At this point, we may have moved into the *engineering culture* again.

6) The final result is congruent with the goals set at the beginning, and we seem to end the process in the culture it started with.

However, R. Bouwen who executed the whole study, concludes that the 'most important quality of the process is the two-sidedness of communication' and the 'continuing consensual decision-making'. (Bouwen e.a., 1991, p.48) If we can accept that, and I see no reason to doubt the author's evaluation, then the whole process - even though it moved at certain moments or episodes back and forth between several cultures - was basically imbedded in a communicative perspective. At some moments in the process - like the "difficult" group discussion - some "engineering" even helped communicative action!

Thus a *dominant culture* can be combined with or temporarily be replaced by another culture, given the specific problems, tasks, and contexts that come into the fore-ground during the process.

The same can be said of other examples given above. Cognitively Guided Instruction, which is clearly situated within the expert culture of education, given its basic curriculum goal of teaching basic mathematics and its school setting - at certain moments leaves the expert culture for the engineering (working with concrete objects) and, especially, for the communicative culture. This happens during the teacher-student and student-student interactions with the common exploration of experiences and the acceptance of different "solutions" for one and the same task. Another example of switching cultures is witnessed in the P.O.M.-project, involving 15 local sections of the KAV-women's movement. It was mainly of the "engineering type", since the top of the movement and the researchers wanted to change members' attitudes and to reverse their local programming practices. But participants clearly moved to the expert culture when analyses of the school system and of parents participation opportunities were made, and it also had its communicative episodes where women explored and expressed their experiences with their own and their daughters' school education at the local level.

As we have seen, K. Staessens found three different types of grammar school cultures in her research of nine schools within the VLO-innovation project in Belgium's Flemish community. (Staessens, 1990). She speaks metaphorically of the "family school", the "school as professional institution" and the "Living-Apart-Together" school. A brief analysis showed that the first two types bear clear similar-ities to the "communicative" and the "engineering culture" respectively. It is interest-ing to note, however, that this researcher was not able to classify one of the schools, apparently because of a lack of empirical interview material. However, in a footnote, she characterises its headmaster as situated somewhere between the "grandfather headmaster" of the family school and the "architect headmaster" of the professional school. 'For me, says one teacher, he is the best director I've had in my whole career.... at both the social, the personal and the pedagogical level'. (o.c. p. 321) Instead of saying that this director is "situated in between two cultures", one could conclude that he has combined or maybe even integrated both of them.

In educational praxis and literature, we sometimes encounter explicit attempts at combining different cultures of education and learning. One of these attempts is the so-called *Theme-Centred-Interaction* theory and practice, initiated by former German psycho-analyst Ruth Cohn. (Cohn, 1969 & 1976). In fact, we should speak here of a practice leading to a theory: the Berlin-born psycho-therapist, being confronted with the horrors of the persecution of her jewish colleagues by the nazis, fled her native country and immigrated to the USA in 1941. There, she met several experientially oriented psycho-analysts and discovered "progressive education", which was an attempt at realising a non-oppressive and non-competitive form of basic school education. She gradually broadened the scope of her person-oriented therapeutic practice to life- and society oriented group work, founded a Workshop Institute for Living Learning, and developed a consistent theory and a method about learning-in-interaction. Even though - like in the case of Freire - her work became known first of all as a "method", it was based on a set of ethical axioms:

(1) The human being is at the same time a psycho-biological unit and an integral part of the universe. A human person is therefore at the same time autonomous and dependent of the universe and the community. Autonomy grows only by the grace of a growing awareness of mutual dependency.

(2) To be human is to respect all that lives and grows, and this implies ethical decisions in favour of development and against violence.

(3) We are limited by internal and external boundaries, but humans can expand these boundaries by their own free decision.

These axioms were translated into a basic model of "Living Learning" as the interaction of three basic poles within a global societal context: individual persons (the I) engage themselves together with others (the WE) in the exploration of a task or theme (the IT), and this "triangle" is situated within the social, economical and political GLOBE, which surrounds it like an active circle. In Cohn's view, to learn is to integrate personal development (I-goals) with group development (We-goals) and task development (Reality goals). The process of learning can be seen as a *dynamic balancing* between these three poles. In fact, as one long-time practitioner and researcher of TCI puts it, one never reaches the perfect balance, but the task is 'to balance the never balanced' (Callens, 1982, p. 29) In order to realise this process, participants, and especially "leaders" should respect a set of two related *postulates*:

(I) "Be your own chair person", i.e. develop yourself according to your needs and those of others, and take adequate decisions;

(Ii) "Disturbances take precedence" or "Reality has authority", i.e. the learning process is inevitably perturbed by tensions or conflicts, which may be related to the individual, the group, the kind of theme dealt with or the outer Globe. It is only by expressing and paying attention at these disturbing factors that persons and groups can develop and grow in efficiency and solidarity.

Furthermore, a set of 10 concrete interaction rules (like 'speak in the I-form, speak for yourself' and 'side talks have priority') ought to help the leader and the group to progress.

The central focus of TCI is the so-called *theme*, which is in fact a specification of an element of the Globe, but at the same time related to the experiential world of each participant and the group as a whole.

Hearing all this, one might conclude that Cohn has developed a kind of group work method, which is still very person-oriented, and belongs to the current of Gestalt, Encounter, etc. That impression is sometimes corroborated by some TCI-training programmes, as I experienced them together with student groups. But that is too narrow an interpretation. Efforts have been made e.g. to apply TCI within schools and professional training centres, especially in those countries where "TCI-societies" are at work, like the Netherlands, and where TCI-based curricula for several courses have been developed.

Anyhow, our brief description may suffice to show that TCI, when projected onto the different cultures of education and learning, is indeed an attempt to combine (elements of) the communicative, the prophetic and the expert culture. One author rightly situates it within Habermas' theory of communicative action, and also links it to critical or emancipatory pedagogy (Van Loosbroek, 1992, p. 176 f.). On the other hand, she detects "modern" as well as "postmodern" elements in it, like the focus on personal autonomy on the one hand and the emphasis on pluriformity or the refusal to believe in definitive "truth" or "blueprints for society" on the other hand. Personally, I see clear links to the example of the Materials case, and situate it ultimately in the communicative culture of education, admitting that it contains more than just an occasional selection of elements from the prophetic and the expert cultures.

An area of practice where attempts at integration of paradigms and cultures has repeatedly been made is that of community organisation. The KREMAB-project described in the third chapter shows an attempt at a "multi-functional" approach at the neighbourhood level. One of the reasons for such attempts is the octopus-like problem of deprivation and poverty to which this type of work often addresses itself. A recent example of a renewed attempt is that of the so-called "integrated basic networks in combatting poverty", emerging from an action-oriented research project in four neighbourhoods in Belgium (Baert & Hellinckx, 1992). In this experimental approach, one works according to a combined set of principles: low threshold of services and small scale, continuous activation of inhabitants, direct participation, multifunctionality, use of individual as well as group methods, preventive personal and structural support. This approach is basically communicative, but bears traits of the expert and engineering cultures as well.

Other examples of combining or even integrating different cultures maybe found in the concept and the method of "project work", as it is practised in several schools and universities. Here too, the study of a "theme" is linked to both the We of the group, the I of the teacher and of each individual student, and the Globe of the educational institution in relation to (parts of) the outside world. Looking at the different forms of practice of this "method" however, one can only conclude that project work sometimes comes down to a combination of the communicative and the expert culture - like in project groups dealing with rather abstract themes and using books as their main sources of information - , or the communicative and the engineering culture - like in projects oriented to concrete structural changes or the realisation of specific action programmes in cooperation with practice organisations.

A last example is closely linked to our own university section of social pedagogy: after ca 15 years of research and teaching, we developed our own theory of the educative process in 1984, as "an open growth system, oriented at personal development and social emancipation". There we tried to link the "task-oriented" dimension of planning and executing an educative process with the "communicative" dimension of facilitator-learner interaction and the "growth dimension" of the development of learners in relation to their social environment. As a Spanish colleague, A. Requejo, remarked, this is an attempt, not to oppose the "ingenería" of instrumental teaching and personal development to the "emancipatory dimension" of interpersonal solidarity, but to combine and maybe integrate both approaches. (Requejo, 1992). In terms of the present book, we seemed to try to combine three cultures: the engineering, the communicative and the prophetic. In the final analysis, the accent is put on "systematic education as a process of trying to convert educative needs into learning results, in common interaction between educators and participants".

The title of this concluding chapter speaks of a four-clover leaf of cultures, providing it with a question mark. The comparative juxtaposition of these four, together with a (renewed) analysis of practical examples and efforts at integration does not lead to an unequivocal confirmation of the "four-in-one" thesis. The four cultures of education and learning stand in their own right, serving their purposes and nourishing their members. Each of them has its merits and its limits, and in some periods and places, they even are combined or used in each other's support. This is a consoling postmodern conclusion. In a society which, as was stated above, balances between trust and risk, safety and insecurity, peace and violence, we simply have no final answer to the question of the "right education". Specific problems, like those of technology, the ecological crisis, the co-habitation of people from different ethnic backgrounds, the organisation of labour, the demands of the labour market, the North-South rift, the search for a nurturing community - require specific answers. Education and learning are no more and no less than a contributing force. In as far as life problems and challenges can be translated into demands for education and learning, specific problems need specific answers. Sometimes they shall be given within one type of culture, sometimes in a combination.

Moreover, educators or learners do not always have a choice of an educative culture: the social and economical context, the institutional organisation of education and local traditions play an important role. But then again, it is consoling to see that one type of institution - like the "school" or "the community centre" or "the vocational training organisation" or "the socio-cultural movement" does not simply coincide with one type of culture. The four preceding chapters bear ample proof to that!

One attempt to create the ultimate integrative theory and culture - called theory of education as communicative action - has only succeeded to convince many an educator at the level of non-empirical abstraction. To state that all education cannot be anything else but intersubjective dialogue is thought-provoking and inspiring, but does not explain the actual variety of cultures and practices "in the field" as well as in "praxis theory".

Let us reformulate this conclusion by using a special kind of imagery and narrative. Remaining within the world of plants, we might replace the image of a clover-field with that of a peculiar orchard. In each of its corner zones, we find a specific type of tree, with a special kind of roots, of branches and leaves, oriented to a particular zone of the sky. The trees are called after their specific fruits: the tree of knowledge, the tree of skilful action, the tree of moral conscience and the tree of dialogue and communality. In the border areas between zones, one finds a few hybrids combining the qualities of different types, and producing mixed fruits. In the middle of the orchard, on a heightened platform, one sees the tree-of-all-fruits, with one big stem and several types of branches, bearing ample fruits. But no one has ever been able to climb it and eat from all its fruits.

An old book, describing this beautiful orchard, narrates that it was inhabited once by a young couple. They were attracted to the tree-of- all-fruits, but at the moment that they wanted to climb it and eat from it, the master of the orchard appeared and expelled them from the central area. Since then they wander from tree to tree, sometimes in hope and sometimes in despair, and eat from time to time. Asked why they keep wandering, they reply: the master of the orchard has promised us to let us own the tree of all fruits, after we will have brought the orchard to its full bloom...

REGISTER OF NAMES

144

BIBLIOGRAPHY (consulted literature)

ARENDT, H. (1967[1], 1987[5]). Vita activa oder vom tätigen Leben [About active life]. München: Piper.

AL KASEY, M. (1984). Youth education in Iraq and Egypt 1920 - 1980. A contribution to comparative education in the Arab region. Leuven, Den Haag: Helicon.

AMBROISE, R. & ABRAHAM, D. (1992). Empowering the poor. A review of the adult education programme of the Andhra Pradesh Social Service Society from 1978-1991. Secunderabad: Vani Press.

ARGYRIS, C. & SCHöN, D. (1987). Learning: A theory of action perspective. New York: Addison-Wesley.

AUSTIN, L. (1962). How to do things with words. Oxford: Clarendon Press.

BADINTER, E. & BADINTER, R. (1988). Condorcet. Un intellectuel en politique [Condorcet, an intellectual in politics]. Paris: Fayard.

BAERT, H. (1982). Diagnose in een proces van vorming en buurtopbouw met kansarm genoemde buurtbewoners [Diagnosis in a process of education and community organisation with so-called underprivileged inhabitants]. Leuven: KU Leuven, Fac. Psych. & Ped. Wet. (unpubl. doct. diss.).

BAERT, H. & HELLINCKX L. (1992, Oct.). Geïntegreerde basisschakels in de armoedebestrijding. Contouren van een methodiek [Integrated basic linkages in combatting poverty]. Welzijns-gids, 5, 1-19.

BALLAUFF, TH. (1985). Lehrer sein einst und jetzt. Auf der Suche nach dem verlorenen Lehrer [To be a teacher, then and now. In search of the lost teacher]. Essen: Neue Deutsche Schule.

BANNING, W. (1959). Lijnen van ontwikkeling. [Lines of development]. In T. TEN HAVE (ed.). Vorming. Handboek voor sociaal-cultureel vormingswerk met volwassenen. [Handbook of general adult education]. Groningen: Wolters.

BAUMAN, Z. (1992). Intimations of postmodernity. London: Routledge.

BECKERS, H.J. (1982). Jugendarbeit und Emanzipation [Youth work and emancipation]. Leuven: KU Leuven, Fac. Psych. & Ped. Wet. (unpubl. doct. diss.).

BECKERS, H.J. (1983). Emanzipation und kirchliche Jugendarbeit [Emancipation and youthwork in the church]. Düsseldorf: Schriftenreihe des Jugendhauses Düsseldorf.

BENNIS, W.G., BENNE, K.D. & CHIN, R. (Eds). (1962). *The planning of change. Readings in applied behavioral sciences.* New York: Holt. (rev. ed. 1968).

BERMAN, P. (1981). Educational change. An implementation paradigm. In R. LEHMING & M. KANE (Eds.), *Improving schools.* (pp. 253-286). London, Beverly Hills: Sage.

BERNSTEIN, B. (1985). *Habermas and modernity.* New York: Basil Blackwell.

BLOCH, E. (1959). *Das Prinzip Hoffnung* [The Principle of Hope]. vol.II. (pp. 819-1657). Frankfurt: Suhrkamp.

BLOOM, B.S. (1956). *Taxonomy of educational objectives. The classification of education. Handbook I: Cognitive domain.* New York: Longmans & Green.

BOCKSTAEL, E. (Ed.). *Handicap et politique* [Handicapped people and politics]. Bruxelles: Equipage Éditions.

BOLHUIS, S. (1988). Leren [Learning]. In B. VAN GENT & A. NOTTEN, *o.c.,* (pp. 69-86).

BOUWEN, R. & FRY, R. (1991). Organizational innovation and learning. Four patterns of dialogue between the dominant logic and the new logic. *Int. Studies of Management and Organization, 21*(4), 37-51.

BOUWEN, R. (1992). De lerende organisatie [The learning organisation]. In K. DE WITTE, K., *Continu opleiden. Integrale opleidingszorg als HRM-strategie.* o.c. (p.61 - 79).

BREZINKA, W. (1981). Die emanzipatorische Pädagogik und ihre Folgen [Emancipatory pedagogy and its consequences]. *Pädagogische Rundschau, 35* (1981), 365-383.

BROOKFIELD, S.D. (1986). *Understanding and facilitating adult learning.* Milton Keynes, Open University, 375p.

BUBER, M. (1923). Ich und Du. In *Das dialogische Prinzip.* Heidelberg, Engl. (1959). *I and Thou.* Edinburgh: T & T Clark.

BUCKLEY, W. (Ed.). (1968). *Modern systems research for the social scientist. A source book.* Chicago: Aldine.

BURGGRAEVE, R. (1981). *Van zelfontplooiing naar verantwoordelijkheid. Een ethische lezing van het verlangen: ontmoeting tussen psychoanalyse en Levinas* [From self-development to responsibility. A confrontation between psychoanalysis and Levinas]. Leuven: Acco.

146

CACÉRES, B. (1964). *Histoire de l'éducation populaire* [History of liberal adult education]. Paris: Seuil.

CALLENS, I. (1982). *Ik, het thema en de anderen* [I, the theme and the others]. Baarn: Nelissen.

CAMMAER, H. (1968). *Jeugd van nu: een zachte generatie* [Today's Youth: a soft generation]. Antwerpen, Utrecht: De Standaard.

CARPENTER, T.P. & FENNEMA, E. (1992). *Cognitively guided instruction: building on the knowledge of students and teachers.* (Manuscr. to appear(Ed.), *The reform of school of mathematics in the United States.* Special issue of the *International Journal of Educational Research.*)

CARTON, M. (1984). *Education and the world of work.* Paris: Unesco (IBE studies and surveys in comparative education).

CLARK, C. (1992). Truth, belief and knowledge. In P. JARVIS (Ed.), *Adult education and theological interpretations*, o.c., (pp. 30-31).

COHN, R. (1969). From couch to circle to community. In H. RUITENBEEK (Ed.), *Group therapy today.* New York: Atherton Press.

COHN, R. (1976). *Von der Psychoanalyse zur themenzentrierten Interaktion* [From Psychoanalysis to theme-centered interaction]. Stuttgart: Klett. Dutch: (1983). *[Van psychoanalyse naar themagecentreerde interaktie.* Baarn: Nelissen].

DE AGUIRRE, P. (1989). *Agogisch handelen in nieuwe sociale bewegingen. Literatuurstudie en verkennend onderzoek van vredesorganisaties.*[Educative action in new social movements. Literature analysis and exploratory research of peace organisations]. Leuven: Fac. Psych. & Ped. Wetensch. (unpubl. doct. diss.).

DE CHAMPEAUX, G. & STERCKX, S. (1964). *Introduction au monde des symboles* [Introduction into the world of symbols].Paris: Weber.

DE CORTE, E., & VAN BOUWEL, J. (1978). Het empirisch onderzoek over de hiërarchisch-cumulatieve structuur van Bloom's taxonomie, cognitief domein: methoden en resultaten [Empirical research on the structure of Bloom's taxonomy]. *Pedagogische Studiën, 55,* 228-239.

DE CORTE, E. e.a. (1988). *Beknopte didaxologie* [Introduction into didactics]. Groningen: Wolters-Noordhoff.

DE DIJN, H. (1991). Post-modernismen: de vlag en de lading , [Postmodernisms: the banner and what it covers]. *Kultuurleven 58* (1991), 19-33.

DE KEYSER, C.C. (1958). *Inleiding in de geschiedenis van het westerse vormings-wezen* [Introduction into the history of the western educational system]. Antwerpen.

DE KEYSER, C.C. (1986). *Naar een comprehensief Europees basisonderwijs voor het jaar 2000.* [Towards a comprehensive European basic education for the year 2000; emeritus lecture]. Leuven: Dep. of Educational Sciences

DE KEYSER, L. (1990). *Het sociaal-cultureel vormingswerk in verenigingsverband: tussen vorming en organisatie* [General adult education in voluntary associations: between education and organisation]. Leuven: Fac. Psych. & Ped. Wet. (unpubl. doct. diss.).

DE KEYSER, L. & VANDEMEULEBROECKE, L. (1992). Educatie alleen is niet genoeg. Een actueel concept van vormingswerk in verenigingsverband [Education is not enough. A concept of general adult education in voluntary associations]. *Vorming,* 7(3), 161-175.

DE MEESTER, P., DILLEMANS, R. a.o. (Red.). (1989). *Wetenschap nu en morgen.* [Science now and tomorrow]. Leuven: Universitaire Pers.

DE MUNTER, A. (1976). *De functie van modellen in de empirisch-pedagogische onderzoekscyclus* [The function of models in empirical educational research]. Leuven: Fac. Psych. & Ped. wet.(unpubl. doct. dissertation).

DEPAEPE, M. (1993). History of education anno 1992: 'A tale told by an idiot, full of sound and fury, signifying nothing?, *History of Education,* 22(1), 1-10.

DERRIDA, J. (1962). *Traduction et introduction à E. Husserl, L'origine de la géométrie* [Translation and introduction to E. Husserl, the origin of geometry]. Paris: Presses Universitaires de France.

DERRIDA, J. (1967). *De la grammatologie.* Paris: Editions de Minuit. Engl. (1976). *On grammatology.* Baltimore: John Hopkins Press.

DE VRIES, (1988). *Het leven en de leer. Een studie naar de verbinding van leren en werken in de stage* [Praxis and theory. A study into the combination of learning and working]. Nijmegen: ITS, (unpubl. doct. diss.).

DE WAELE, A., DOUTERLUNGNE, M. & COSSEY, H. (1985). *Tussen school en werkbank. Deeltijds leren bij 15-18 jarigen* [Between the school and the workfloor. Part-time education of 15-18 year olds]. Brussel: CED Samson.

DEWILDE, J., JONNIAUX, F. & LOMBAERT, G. *Opvoeding tot ontwikkelingssamenwerking* [Education towards development]. Leuven: Fac. Psych. & Ped. (unpubl. M.A. Thesis).

148

DESHLER, D. (1992). Prophecy: Radical adult education and the politics of power. In P. JARVIS (Ed.), *Adult education and theological interpretations*. o.c., (pp. 272 - 308).

DEWEY, J. (1938). *Experience and education*. London: Collier-Macmillan.

DE WITTE, K. (Ed.). (1992). *Continu opleiden. Integrale kwaliteitszorg als HRM-strategie* [Continuous professional training. Integral quality control as HRM-strategy]. Leuven: Acco.

ELIAS, J.L. & MERRIAM, S. (1980). *Philosophical foundations of adult education*. Malabar: Robert E. Krieger.

FACHÉ, W. (1992). De beleidsontwikkelende en participatieve Delphi methode [The policy-developing and participatory Delphi method]. In W. LEIRMAN, W. FACHÉ, e.a. *Educatie 92* o.c. (pp. 106 - 121).

FAURE, E., e.a. (1973). *Apprendre à Etre - Learning to Be*. Paris: Unesco.

FENNEMA, E., CARPENTER, T.P. & FRANKE, M.L. (1993). *Cognitively Guided Instruction*, National Center for Research in Mathematical Sciences Education. (unpubl. paper).

FLECHA, R. (1993). *The theory of communicative action and adult education*. Barcelona (unpubl. paper).

FOUCAULT, M. (1966). *Les mots et les choses. Une archéologie des sciences humaines* [On words and things. The archeology of the human sciences]. Paris: Gallimard.

FOUCAULT, M. (1975). *Surveiller et punir. Naissance de la prison* [To guard and to punish. The birth of the prison]. Paris: Gallimard

FREIRE, P. (1969). *La educación como practica de la libertad* [Education as practice of liberty]. Montevideo: Tierra nueva.

FREIRE, P. (1970). *Pedagogía del oprimido*. Montevideo: Tierra nueva. Transl. into English: (1972). *Pedagogy of the oppressed*. Harmondsworth: Penguin. Dutch: (1972). *Pedagogie van de onderdrukten*. Baarn: In Den Toren.

FREIRE, P. (1972). *Cultural action for freedom*. Harmondsworth: Penguin

GAGE, N. L.(Ed). (1963). *Handbook of research on teaching*. Chicago: Rand McNally.

GAGE, N. L. (1992). The paradigm wars and their aftermath. A 'historical' sketch of Research on teaching since 1969. *Educational Researcher*, 18, Oct., 4 - 10.

GALTUNG, J. (1973). Eine strukturelle Theorie des Imperialismus [A structural theory of imperialism]. In J. GALTUNG, *Imperialismus und strukturelle Gewalt. Analysen über abhängige Reproduktion.* Frankfurt/Main: Suhrkamp.

GIDDENS, A. (1990). *The consequences of modernity.* Cambridge: Cambridge University Press.

GIESECKE, H. (1973). *Bildungsreform und Emanzipation* [Educational reform and emancipation]. München: Juventa.

GIRARD, R. (1978). *Des choses cachées depuis la fondation du monde* [On things hidden since the foundation of the world]. Paris: Grasset.

GRATTAN, H.C. (1955). *In quest of knowledge.* New York: Association Press.

GUBA, E.G. & CLARK, D.L., (1965). *An examination of potential change roles in education.* Washington: Eric.

HABERMAS, J. (1968). *Erkenntnis und Interesse.* Frankfurt/Main: Suhrkamp. (Engl. (1971). *Knowledge and human interests.* Boston: Beacon Press.)

HABERMAS, J. (1982). *Theorie des kommunikativen Handelns.Bd 1: Handlungsrationalität und gesellschaftliche Rationalisierung. Bd 2: Zur Kritik der funktionalistischen Vernunft* [Theory of communicative action. 1: Action rationality and social rationalisation. 2: A criticism of functional rationality.].

HALL, B. (1975). Participatory Research: an approach for change. *Convergence,* 8 (1975), 24 - 32.

HARTFIEL, G. (ed.) (1975). *Emanzipation: ideoligischer Fetisch oder reale Chance?* [Emancipation: ideological fetish or real opportunity ?]. Opladen: Westdeutscher Verlag.

HAVELOCK, R. e.a. (1969). *A comparative study of the literature on the dissemination and utilization of scientific knowledge.* Ann Arbor: Michigan University Press.

HELLEMANS, M. (1976). Wat betekent emancipatie? [What does emancipation mean?). In C.C. DE KEYSER e.a., *De mens zichzelf een taak. Liber amicorum A. Kriekemans.* [*Man: a task onto himsel]* Tielt, Amsterdam: Lannoo.

HELLEMANS, M. & DE CLERCK, K. (Eds). (1988). *Wegwijzer: over de leerkracht als referentiefiguur* [Guide-post: the teacher as reference figure]. Leuven: KU Leuven, Centrum voor Fundamentele Pedagogiek.

HERNANDEZ, J. (1977). *Pädagogik des Seins: Paulo Freires praktische Theorie einer emanzipatorischen Erwachsenenbildung* [Pedagogy of Being: Paulo Freire's practical theory of emancipatory adult education]. Lollar: Achenbach.

150

HINNEKINT, H. (1984). *Perspectieven voor de volwasseneneducatie. Een bundel concepten en modellen voor de uitbouw van de volwassenenvorming in de toekomst* [Perspectives for adult education]. Antwerpen: Van Loghum Slaterus.

HUTJES, J.M. (1985). Beleidsonderzoek in de jaren tachtig, een poging tot een balans [Policy research in the 1980's: an attempt at evaluation]. In BERENDS e.a. (Eds.), *Sociologisch Jaarboek*. Deventer.

IMAI, M. (1986). *Kaizen: the key to Japanese competitive success*. New York: Random House . Dutch: (1990). *Kaizen*. Antwerpen: Kluwer.

JALLADE, J. (1982). *Alternierende Ausbildung für Jugendliche. Leitfaden für Praktiker* [Dual Education for youngsters. A guideline for practitioners]. Berlin: Cedefop.

JALLADE, J. (1988). *La formation professionnelle à l'étranger, quels enseignements pour la France ?* [Vocational Education in foreign countries, what lessons for France ?]. Paris: Univ. de Paris IX, Commissariat Général du Plan.

JANSEN, T. & KLERCQ, J. (1992). Experiential learning and modernity. In D. WILDEMEERSCH e.a. (Eds). *Adult education, experiential learning and social change*. o.c., 93 - 104.

JARVIS, P. (Ed.). (1993). *Adult education and theological interpretations*. Malabar (Fl.): Krieger.

JARVIS, P. (Ed.). (1987). *Twentieth century thinkers in adult education*. London: Croom Helm.

JOUSSELIN, J. (1966). *Une nouvelle jeunesse française* [A new French youth generation]. Toulouse: Privat.

KAYZER, W. (Ed.). (1993). *Een schitterend ongeluk*. [A Glorious accident]. Amsterdam, Antwerpen: Contact. (Publication of TV-interviews and group discussion with O. Sachs, S. Gould, S. Toulmin, D.Dennett, R. Sheldrake & F. Dyson).

KOLB, D.A., (1984). *Experiential learning: experience as the source of learning and development*. Engelwood Cliffs, Prentice Hall.

KUNNEMAN, H. (1983). *Habermas' theorie van het communicatieve handelen* [Habermas' theory of communicative action]. Meppel: Boom.

LACAN, J. (1966). *Le stade du miroir comme formateur de la fonction du Je* [The stadium of the mirror as constituent of the I function].In *Écrits*, I., Paris: Ed. du Seuil.

LAEVERS, F. (1991). *The innovative project experiential education.* Leuven: CEO.

LEIRMAN, W. (1971). Het project Onderwijs voor Meisjes: van opinie- naar actie-onderzoek [The project Education for girls: from attitude to action research]. Leuven: *Tijdschrift voor Opvoedkunde, 17*(3,5). (reprint).

LEIRMAN, W. (1976). Jeugd en emancipatie. Overzicht en konklusies uit een diagnose-onderzoek 1974-'75' [Youth and emancipation: review and conclusions of a diagnostic survey]. *Jeugd en Samenleving, 6* (1976), 164-194.

LEIRMAN, W., BAERT, H. & VERBEKE, L. (1980). Het aktie-onderzoek "Kreativiteit en emancipatie in een buurt" in het licht van deontologie en etiek [The action-research project KREMAB in the light of ethics]. *Verslagboek driedaags colloquium Aktie-Onderzoek.* Brussel: Programmatie Wetenschapsbeleid.

LEIRMAN, W. & KULICH, J. (Eds.). (1987). *Adult education and the challenges of the 1990's.* London: Croom Helm. (Nl: (1987). *Vormingswerk en de uitdagingen van de jaren '90.* Leuven: Acco.

LEIRMAN, W. (1988). Opvoeden in crisistijd [To educate]. *Leuvens Bulletin LAPP, 24*(5), 146-155.

LEIRMAN, W. (1992). Maatschappelijke uitdagingen voor het sociaal-cultureel werk anno 1992: de netto-waarde van mens en natuur [Social challenges for general adult education anno 1992]. In D. WILDEMEERSCH, & J. GOUBIN (Eds.), *Het vormingswerk uitgedaagd.* Mechelen: VCVO.

LEIRMAN, W., FACHÉ, W, GEHRE G., JACOBS I., VERHAERT C., VAN DAMME D.,e.a. (1992). *EDUCATIE '92 : onderzoek naar een behoeftendekkend aanbod en een beter gecoördineerd beleid inzake permanente vorming in Vlaanderen. (Eindrapport)* [Project Education '92: final report, with partial Engl. transl.]. Leuven, Gent: KU Leuven - RU Gent, 1992.

LEIRMAN W., ETUDIANTS 3ème LICENCE FOPA, *EDUCATION PERMANENTE '92.Vers une offre couvrant les nécessités et une politique d'éducation permanente mieux coordinée en Communauté Française.* Louvain-La-Neuve: Fopa.

LEIRMAN, W. & ANCKAERT, L. (1992). Moral issues in adult education: from life problems to educational goals and postmodern uncertainty. In P. JARVIS, (Ed.), *Adult education and theological interpretations,* o.c. (pp. 259-272).

LESNE, M. (1977). *Travail pédagogique et formation d'adultes.* [Pedagogical work and training of adults] Paris: PUF.

LEVINAS, E. (1961). *Totalité et Infini. Essai sur l'exteriorité* [Totality and Infinity. An Essay on exteriority]. The Hague: Nijhoff.

152

LEVINAS, E. (1972). *Humanisme de l'autre homme* [Humanism of the other man]. Montpellier: Fata Morgana.

LINDEBOOM, M. & PETERS, J.J. (1986). *Didactiek voor opleiders in organisaties* [Didactics for trainers in organisations]. Deventer: Van Loghum Slaterus.

LIPPITT, R., WATSON, J. & WESTLEY, B. (1958). *The dynamics of planned change*. New York: Harcourt.

LOVETT, T. (1988). *Radical adult education: a reader*. London: Routledge.

LOWYCK, J. (1992). Didactische maatregelen in arbeidsorganisaties. [Didactical measures in labour organisations] in K. DE WITTE (ed.), *Continu opleiden, o.c.*, [Continuous professional training] pp. 81-98.

LYOTARD, J.F. (1979). *La condition postmoderne. Rapport sur le savoir*. Paris: Éditions de Minuit. (Engl. (1984). *The postmodern condition*. Minneapolis: Univ. of Minnesota Press.

Mc CAFFRY, T. (1993). The Priesthood of the teacher and the teaching of the word. In P. JARVIS (Ed.), *Adult education and theological interpretations*. o.c., (pp. 53-66.).

MAGER, R. F. (1975). *Preparing instructional objectives*. Belmont (Cal.) Fearon.

MARCUSE, H. (1969). *Versuch über die Befreiung* [On Liberation]. Frankfurt: Suhrkamp (transl. from English).

MARSICK, V. (1987). *Learning in the workplace*. London: Croom Helm.

MASSCHELEIN, J. (1987). *Pedagogisch handelen en communicatief handelen. De 'ontbinding' van het opvoedingsbegrip en de betekenis van Habermas' "kommunikationstheoretische Wende" voor de pedagogiek*. [Educative and communicative action. The 'dissolution' of the concept of education and the meaning of the "switch to communication theory" by Habermas for educational science]. Leuven: KU Leuven, Fac. Psych. & Ed. (n. publ. doct. diss.).

MASSCHELEIN, J. (1991) Zijn er nog overlevingskansen voor het 'Bildungsideal'? Pleidooi voor vorming die niet 'werkt' en niets 'verbetert' [Can the ideal of 'Bildung' survive? A playdoyer in favour of education which does not 'work' or try to 'optimize']. *Vorming*, 7(1), 39-52.

MANNHEIM, K. (1941). *Man and society in an age of reconstruction*. New York: Harcourt & Brace.

MATTHEEUWS, A. (1977). Systeembenadering en kommunikatietheorieën [Systems approach and communication theory]. In *Leren en leven met groepen*,4110, 1-33.

153

MEADOWS, D. e.a. (1972). *The limits to growth. A report for the Club of Rome's project on the predicament of mankind.* New York: Universe.

MESDOM, F. & WIELEMANS, W. (1978). 'Het systeemdenken in de onderwijskunde. Een oriëntatie' [Systems theory in school education. An orientation]. *Pedagogisch Tijdschrift*, 3(10), 541-565.

MEZIROW, J. (1975). *Education for perspective transformation: Women's re-entry programs in Community Colleges.* New York: Center for Adult Education.

MEZIROW, J. (1978). Perspective transformation, *Adult Education (8)*, 100-110.

MEZIROW, J. (1981). A critical theory of adult education, *Adult Education*, 32, 3 - 24.

MEZIROW, J. (1991). *Transformative dimensions of adult education.* San Francisco: Jossey-Bass.

MOLLENHAUER, KL. (1968). *Erziehung und Emanzipation* [Education and emancipation]. München: Juventa.

MOSER, H. (1975). *Aktionsforschung als kritische Theorie der Sozialwissenschaften* [Action research as critical theory of the social sciences]. München: Kösel.

NEGT, O. (1975). *Soziologische Phantasie und exemplarisches lernen. Zur Theorie und Praxis der Arbeiterbildung* [Sociological phantasy and exemplary learning. Contribution to the theory of workers' education]. München: Europäische Verlagsanstalt. 1971[1].

NUTTIN, J. (1962). *Psycho-analyse en spiritualistische opvatting van de mens.* Antwerpen: Standaard.

PERLS, F. & HEFFERLINE, R., GOODMAN, P. (1968). *Gestalt therapy.* Harmondsworth: Penguin.

PETERSON, G. A. (Ed). (1984). *The christian education of adults.* Chicago: Moody Press.

PILLAI, M. (1979). *Let my country awake.* Secunderabad: APPSS.

PÖGGELER, F. & B. WOLTERHOFF.(Eds). (1981). *Neue Theorien der Erwachsenenbildung.* [New theories of adult education] Stuttgart: Kohlhammer.

PROSMANS, K. (1992). *Het autonoom pedagogisch team als schakel in het alternerend leren in de leertijd.* [The autonomous pedagogical team as linkage in the dual learning system]. KU Leuven, Fac. of Psych. and Educ. Sciences, (unpublished thesis).

154

PULI, A. (1988). *Adult education and people-centered development. Analysis and case studies in the state of Andhra Pradesh, India.* Leuven: KU Leuven, Fac. Psych. & Ped. Wet. (n. publ. doct. diss.).

REE, H., (1971). *Educator extraordinary: the life and achievement of Henry Morris 1889-1961.* London: Longmans.

REQUEJO, A. (1992). *Educación de adultos como proceso.* [Adult education as a process]. El Correo Gallego, 13-9-92.

ROGERS, E. (1983). *Diffusion of innovations.* New York: The Free Press.

ROGERS, E. & SHOEMAKER, (1971). *Communication of innovations. A cross-cultural approach.* New York: The Free Press.

RÖSSNER, L. (1973). Kritische Pädagogik und die Zielproblematik in der Erziehung [Critical pedagogy and the problematic of educational objective]. *Die Deutsche Schule,* 65 (1973), 447 - 464.

SALGADO, J. (1985). *Alfabetisación en America Latina en su contexto internacional. Estudio comparado de los casos de Brasil, Chile, Mexico y Nicaragua* [Literacy Education in Latin America. A comparative study of Brasil, Chile, Mexico and Nicaragua]. Leuven: KU Leuven, Fac. Psych. & Ped. Wet. (n. publ. doct. diss.).

SALGADO, J. & LEIRMAN, W. (1987). Basic adult education in Latin America: the case of Mexico in comparison to Brasil, Chile and Nicaragua. In J. KNOLL (Ed.), *International Yearbook of adult education:* Vol. 15 (pp. 33-48).

SCIENTIA PEDAGOGICA EXPERIMENTALIS (1988) *Topical values in education,* Gent, 520 p. (Special issue)

SCHÄFTER, O. (1981). *Zielgruppenorientierung in der Erwachsenenbildung. Aspekte einer erwachsenenpädagogischen Planungs- und Handlungskategorie* [Target group orientation in adult education]. Braunschweig: Westermann.

SCHEIN, E.H. (1969). *Process consultation: its role in organisation development.* Reading M.A: Addison-Wesley.

SMEYERS, P. (1992). Pedagogiek op de grens van een nieuw zelfbewustzijn [Educational sciences on the border of a new self-consciousness]. *Leuvens Bulletin LAPP,* 60(2), 149 - 176.

STALPERS, J. (1981). 'Wetenschap en praktijk: drie wijzen van denken om menselijke problemen op te lossen' [Science and practice: three ways to solve human problems]. In W. LEIRMAN & L. VANDEMEULEBROECKE, *Vormingswerk en vormingswetenschap. Een agologisch handboek. I.* [Adult education in theory and practice] Leuven: Helicon.

STAESSENS, K. (1990). *De professionele cultuur van basisscholen in vernieuwing. Een empirisch onderzoek in V.L.O.-scholen* [The professional culture of innovating grammar schools].Leuven: KU Leuven, Centrum voor Onderwijsbeleid en -vernieuwing. (doct. dissertation).

TEILHARD DE CHARDIN, P. (1955). *Le phénomène humain* [Man as a phenomenon]. Paris: Éditions du Seuil.

TODD, A.K., & MARTIN, P. (1986). The Alberta Adult Basic Education Project. In W. LEIRMAN (Ed.), *Adult Education and the Challenges of the 1990's (Project-presentations)* (pp 230 - 243). K.U. Leuven: Afdeling Sociale Pedagogiek.

VAN AVERMAET, E. (1988). *De sociale psychologie van het vijanddenken.* [Social psychology of enimical thinking]. Brussel: M.W.T.A. (verslagboek colloquium 17.10.87).

VAN CROMBRUGGE, H., (1992). Opvoeden na Hiroshima [To educate after Hiroshima. The bottomless existence: not an abstract idea, but a concrete fact]. *Vorming 7(5).*

VAN DAMME, D. (1992). Het overheidsbeleid uitgedaagd door het sociaal-cultureel werk of omgekeerd? [Does general adult education challenge public policy, or is the reverse the case?] In WILDEMEERSCH, D. & J. GOUBIN (ed) *Sociaal-cultureel werk en overheidsbeleid vandaag. Deel 1.* Mechelen: VCVO.

VANDEMEULEBROECKE, L. (1977). *Het Project Onderwijs voor Meisjes. Analyse en theorievorming omtrent opzet en verloop van een vormingsproces in een sociaal-culturele vereniging* [The Project Education for Girls: analysis of the educative process]. Leuven: KU Leuven, Fac. Psych. & Education, I-II. (unpubl. doct. dissert.).

VANDENBERG, R.M. & VANDENBERGHE, R. (1981). *Onderwijsinnovatie in verschuivend perspectief* [Educational innovation in a changing perspective]. Tilburg: Zwijssen.

VANDENBERGHE, R. & DEPOORTERE, J. (Eds). (1986). *Het V.L.O.-project in Vlaanderen. Van plan naar realiteit* [The V.L.O.-project in Flanders. From plan to realisation]. Leuven: Acco.

VAN DER VEEN, R. (1982). *Aktivering in opbouw- en vormingswerk.* [Activating participants in community organisation and adult education]. Baarn: Nelissen.

VAN DER VEEN, R. (1992). Foundations of community education and the danger of "aesthetisicism". In P. JARVIS (Ed.), *Adult education and theological interpretations.* o.c. (pp. 187 - 201).

VAN GENT, B. & NOTTEN, A. (Eds) (1988). *Inleiding tot de volwasseneneducatie* [Introduction to adult education]. Meppel: Boom.

156

VAN LOOSBROEK, L. (1992). Cohn's theme-centered interaction (TCI) and critical pedagogy. In D. WILDEMEERSCH & T. JANSEN, *Adult education, experiential learning and social change*. o.c. (pp. 169 - 181).

VAN MOEN, F. (1984). *"Ontscholing van de maatschappij" versus "educatieve samenleving": een studie van het Russisch en westers ontscholingsdenken en zijn kritisch-utopische draagwijdte* ["Deschooling society" versus "educative society"]. Leuven: KU Leuven, Fac. Psych. & Ped. Wet. (unpubl. doct. diss.).

VAN ONNA, B. (1985). *Arbeid als leersituatie* [The workplace as a learning situation]. In G. KRAAYVANGER & B. VAN ONNA (Ed), *Arbeid en leren. Bijdragen tot de volwasseneneducatie. Nelissen*.

VAN ONNA, B. (1992). *Adult education, the labour market and the workplace*. Barcelona: Univ. de Barcelona (unpubl. Lectures in he framework of an international Erasmus Programme).

VERBEKE, L. (1977). 'Het aktie-onderzoek Jeugd en Emancipatie'. In MINISTERIE NEDERLANDSE CULTUUR, (Ed.), *Van onderzoek tot jeugdbeleid* [From youth research to youth policy]. Leuven: Acco, 1977. (Action-research Youth and Emancipation)

VON HENTIG, H. (1975). *Cuernavaca oder: Alternativen zur Schule?* [Cuernavaca: an alternative to the school system ?]. Stuttgart: Klett.

WELTEN, V. e.a. (1973). *Jeugd en emancipatie* [Youth and emancipation]. Bilthoven: Ambo.

WIELEMANS, W. (1993). *Voorbij het individu: mensbeelden in wetenschappen* [Beyond the individual: images of man in the sciences]. Leuven: Garant.

WEIL, S. & McGILL, I. (1989). *Making sense of experiential learning. Diversity in theory and practice*. Milton Keynes: Open University Press.

WILDEMEERSCH, D. & JANSEN, T. (Eds). (1992). *Adult education, experiential learning and social change. The postmodern challenge*. Den Haag: Vuga.

WILDEMEERSCH, D. & LEIRMAN, W. (1989). The facilitation of lifeworld-transformation. *Adult Education Quarterly*, 39, 19-30.
WILDEMEERSCH, D. & GOUBIN, J. (Eds). (1992). *Het vormingswerk uitgedaagd* [Challenges to socio-cultural adult education]. Mechelen: VCVO.

ZANGERLE, I. (1986). *Geschichtsrichtig handeln lernen. Zur Diskussion über Inhalte der Erwachsenenbildung* [Learn how to act in accordance with history: the discussion of contents of adult education]. In A. BENNING (Ed.), *Erwachsenenbildung. Bilanz und Zukunftperspektiven* (Festschrift for F. PÖGGELER) (pp. 198 - 224). Paderborn: Schöningh.

Studien zur Pädagogik, Andragogik und Gerontagogik

Herausgeber: Franz Pöggeler

The State and Adult Education
Historical and Systematical Aspects
Edited by Franz Pöggeler

Frankfurt/M., Berlin, Bern, New York, Paris, Wien 1990. 486 pp.,
6 fig., 2 tab.
Studies in Pedagogy, Andragogy and Gerontology. Vol. 4
General Editor: Franz Pöggeler
ISBN 3-631-42011-0   pb. DM 105.--

Most of the contributions to this anthology deal with various problems
in the relationship between the State and Adult Education past and
present. Particular attention is paid to individual states or political
regions in Europe, Asia, Africa and America. The volume also
presents, however, papers on general aspects such as the role of Adult
Education with regard to wars, revolutions, political conflicts and
ways of political and governmental influence on Adult and Further
Education.

Contents: Contributions by Y. Ambroise, J. Antochi, M. Boucouva-
las, L. Bown, M. Brown, A. Bron-Wojciechowska, J. Field, R. Field-
house, M. Friedenthal-Haase, K. Garnitschnig, M. R. Hellyer,
P. G. H. Hopkins, P. Jarvis, P. Keane, J. H. Knoll, K. Künzel, W. Leir-
man, H. B. Long, K. Miyasaka, H. Möhle, M. Omolewa, F. Pöggeler,
P. Röhrig, R. Rohfeld, B. Samolovcev, I. Savicky, S. Shimada,
V. Skovgaard-Petersen, D. W. Stewart, H. Stubblefield, E. Turay,
L. Turos, M. Usui, M. R. Welton, M. Yamaguchi, K. Yaron, P. Yrjölä,
H. Zdarzil.

Verlag Peter Lang Frankfurt a.M. · Berlin · Bern · New York · Paris · Wien
Auslieferung: Verlag Peter Lang AG, Jupiterstr. 15, CH-3000 Bern 15
Telefon (004131) 9411122, Telefax (004131) 9411131
‒ Preisänderungen vorbehalten ‒